BOSNIAN IMMIGRANTS

OPPORTUNITIES AND CHALLENGES IN THE GREATER ROCHESTER AREA

Aiša Purak

Cover Design by Nihad Talić
Interior Design by Nihad Talić

Translation by Merjema Purak

Printed by CreateSpace,
An Amazon.com Company

CreateSpace Independent Publishing Platform,
North Charleston, SC.

II

TABLE OF CONTENTS

IV

LIST OF ILLUSTRATIVE MATERIALS

VIII

DEDICATION

This research paper is dedicated to my late parents Hurmo and Saliha Bećirović, both for their encouragement and their endless support. My father imparted to me a sense of love, passion, and curiosity towards knowledge. He used to tell me, "When you have open hands, you can give and receive blessings, but if your hands are closed, you can neither receive nor give a blessing that goes around." Throughout my life, I have fol- lowed my father's advice. Irrespective of what I had to offer to my close family, extended family, friends, and community, I always did what I could do to the best of my ability. Indeed, my father's inspiration prompted me to do volunteer work in my Bosnian community, patiently producing amazing results, while still caring for and supporting my extended family in Bosnia and Herzegovina. In the same way, my mother's love for humankind was unparalleled. As an orphan herself—her mother had died when she was just a baby—so she understood what it meant to lead life without love. She always gave what she lacked during her childhood, love and empathy to all those around her. She loved both, my siblings and myself unconditionally, and for that, I miss her most profoundly.

x

ACKNOWLEDGMENTS

I would like to extend my thanks and appreciation to Dr. Salahuddin Malik for his continued encouragement and guidance throughout my Master's Degree program at The Department of History of the College-at Brockport, State University of New York. Dr. Malik has been an integral part of my Master's Degree program because of his continuous encouragement and motivation. He advised me to become fearless and not to cower in the face of hard work and new challenges. Additionally, he allowed me to be a part of his one-of-a-kind project for the region entitled: "History of the Islamic Center of Rochester and Ethnic Muslim Communities it serves." This inspired me to start my own project, entitled "History of Bosnian Immigrants in the Greater Rochester Area." The skills I developed throughout my collaboration with Dr. Malik while working on his project and under his supervision helped me tremendously, not only with completing my Master's Degree, but also with my later research endeavors and publications. Once again, Dr. Malik helped shape my academic identity which enabled me to open doors of endless opportunities. He also helped and encouraged me to turn my research into a book not only because of the importance with the issues Bosnian refugees faced in Rochester, but also to underline the endless opportunities offered to Bosnian refugees in America.

I am grateful for the love, support and encouragement that both my husband Midhat and my daughters Amina and Merjema provided me throughout this project. I also wish to express my sincere thanks to my dear friend Daniel Haug, who selflessly helped me to complete this research. Additionally, I want to thank all the men and women from my Bosnian community in Rochester, New York, who graciously agreed to share their experiences and participate in my research. Specifically with the process of gathering valuable material for this research: spending time with Bosnian community members, collecting data and inter- viewing participants, many of whom were refugees who volunteered to share their life stories. I was honored and blessed to be part of their life journey and without their help, this research would not have been possible. I also would like to extend my gratitude to Dr. Katherine Clark for her help, suggestions, and guidelines on this project.

FOREWORD

The work titled *History of Bosnian Immigrants in the Greater Rochester Area* by Aiša Purak has been the result of a long-term theoretical and empirical study, in which the subject being very complex and constantly evolving. Ten social phenomena are the subjects of study, connected, conditioned, and interdependent: Refugees from Srebrenica and Concentration Camps, Rape as an Act of Genocide in Bosnia and Herzegovina from 1992-1995, History of Bosnia and Herzegovina, Who are Bosniaks, Roots of Bosnian Immigrants in America, Generational Gap among Bosnian Immigrants, Bosnian Refugees in America-Background, Bosnian Refugees in Rochester NY, History of Bosnian Organization in Rochester, NY, Culture and Religious Identity of Bosnian Refugees in Rochester, NY.

This research study has utilized all relevant, valid, and reliable sources of data. Gathered information are sufficient, valid, and reliable for defining qualitative determinants and features of phenomena and their mutual relations, including quantitative dimensions, their distribution, and duration. By linking data from the original social research with the findings from the existing pool Purak, set up logical conclusions meaningfully drawn from her findings. The book aims to establish Bosniaks as a natural part of American society. The book goes into psychological precepts of identity development and it does an excellent job illustrating that "identity" is never a homogeneous, one dimensional entity; it is a complex tapestry of background, experience, and individual differences. The book focuses on integration models and presents the way Bosniaks are an integral part of American society. Reading the book gives you a greater appreciation of the blessing of American society and the ease with which groups of all faiths and backgrounds maintain their culture and ancestral identity and simultaneously take on a new identity as Americans. Scientific results, presented in this research paper, represent the pertinent and relevant contribution to the development of scientific findings in the area of social and humanist sciences.

Aiša Purak had the misfortune of sharing this destiny with me and with many others now American citizens, who fled to the USA to escape ethnic cleansing during the 1992-1995 aggression on Bosnia and Herzegovina. Aiša Purak is an exceptional example among the many survivors because she refused to surrender to the challenges that come with that life experience and instead opted to continue pursuing her education in the USA and making various contributions for the betterment of the larger society. Her intellectual contributions on public policy issues concerning vulnerable population groups in the USA are a source of pride in our community. Her public policy advising on issues related to public administration in the USA played an integral part in our long campaign to have the USA join the international community in formally recognizing the genocide that occurred in Bosnia and Herzegovina and establishing July 11 as a Srebrenica Remembrance Day, to honor the victims of Srebrenica massacre.

Aiša Purak now serves as a valuable International Expert Team Council Member with our Institute for Research of Genocide where we work on raising awareness about the tragic events that took place, primarily, but not exclusively, in Bosnia and Herzegovina, which involved gross violations of human rights and unresolved war crimes carried out in Bosnia and Herzegovina from 1992 to 1995.

Dr. Emir Ramić,
Chairman of the Institute for Research of Genocide Canada
Hamilton, Ontario, Canada, January 16. 2017.

PREFACE

I would like to begin my story with some background information and personal journey from a small and beautiful village in Bosnia and Herzegovina to the United States of America. Additionally, I would like my readers to know why I decided to write about the Bosnian Muslim community here in the Greater Area of Rochester, New York. It seems important to document not only the challenges Bosnians experienced coming to a foreign county, but also discovering endless opportunities in the United States of America. These unique opportunities are available to everyone regardless of background, race, age, gender, opportunities that can truly be found only in America. Today, after more than twenty years living in America, overcoming countless obstacles, many Bosnians are living their dream and reaching for their God given potentials while helping their extended families in Bosnia.

Like many other refugees from Bosnia, I fled the Balkans to save both my daughter's life and my own. I was forced to leave my home to seek refuge beyond the borders of my beloved country. After the unforgettable journey and hardship, migrating from one place to an unknown other, I finally arrived in Austria, whereI lived for a year with my daughter. My husband managed to come and visit me and our daughter in Austria. Since my husband was not able to return to Bosnia and Herzegovina, we decided to move to Germany where my in-laws were staying. I lived and worked in Germany for seven years, while supporting my family in Bosnia who were in desperate need of my assistance.

My long and arduous journey ultimately brought me to the United States of America, On December 17th, 1998, with my husband and my two daughters, I arrived in Rochester, NY from Germany, where we lived as refugees for several years. As many other Bosnian refugees who lived in Germany during the start of the aggression on Bosnia and Herzegovina, I could either return to Bosnia or move abroad, to either Canada, Australia or America. In November 1998, I went to Bosnia to seek advice from my mother and my family who were still there, having never left. I could come back to Bosnia and face the myriad obstacles in the post-war country, or once again move to a foreign country. My beloved mother told me: "I love you and I miss you all of the time. I also have a feeling that I will not see you again, but go somewhere else; don't return to Bosnia. The war ended, but the country is torn apart. Your brothers are not working and I don't have any income; at least when you are outside Bosnia, you can help us out and we will have the hope that someone will take care of us." It was a hard decision to make, but I knew my mother had a point.

That was the last time I saw my mother. She passed away on June 10, 2000. With the passing of my mother and, my father having passed away many years before, I felt like an orphan, even as an adult, married and with two kids. Both parents were my motivation and inspiration. Losing them while living in a foreign country as a refugee and not being able to attend their funerals hurt me deeply. It was extremely hard on me to keep motivated after my mother's death. With a broken, but firm heart, I decided to go to the United States where there was potential to help my family. That aspiration has kept me moving ever since.

Because I already had a cousin living in Rochester, the wonderful Zineta Hamzić, with her great husband Zijad Hamzić, who had already sent us an invitation letter to come to Rochester, we ended up in Rochester, NY. My cousins and my host family Zineta and Zijad were very helpful along with my other cousin Izeta Hamzić and her husband Hazim. Their generous sister in law, Halima Stenklić, with her husband Esad, offered to let us stay in their apartment, until we found our own place. They all helped us settle down and complete the necessary paper work. I am very grateful for their help and support. As with many other refugees coming to Rochester, I was also given the choice between immediately finding work and earning some money, which my family in Bosnian desperately needed. The other option was to go to school to learn English and valuable skills that would make my life in America easier. Because I already lived in Germany, I knew that learning English and basic skills would be crucial for my future in America. I would then be better equipped to help my family and my community. Thus, I started to learn English by going to the Family Learning Center where many refugees from different parts of the world came to learn English. That was the first time I had met people from different parts of the world; all with different ethnic backgrounds, languages, cultures, religions etc. It was a new and rewarding experience. Throughout the school, I also had the opportunity to meet Bosnians from different parts of Bosnia and Herzegovina. Even though the majority of Bosnian refugees were Muslim, there was a huge difference between us. Some refugees had more education than others, some were more religious than others, while some others came from cities and some from rural areas and some still were very nostalgic toward the former Yugoslavia.

The Bosnian community in Rochester, even from the early days, in one way or another, was interconnected; they stayed connected through different sports or cultural clubs. However, when I came to Rochester, I noted that Bosnian refugees were not formally organized in any way. They did, however, still gather mostly for children birthdays, weddings, and holiday celebrations. When it came to religious gatherings, they relied primarily on a Turkish mosque and the Islamic Center of Rochester. For Jummah, the Friday prayer, obligatory prayer for every adult man, they would go to theTurkish mosque. During Ramadan, the month of fasting, Bosnians went to a Turkish mosque for dinner and prayer, although a few went to the Islamic Center of Rochester. Bosnians always felt more comfortable with Turks and their mosque, primarily because of their European roots and common culture.

With my cousins, I also went to the Turkish mosque and met their Imam with whom I talked about Bosnian kids and Sunday school for our kids. We agreed that I would inform and encourage Bosnian parents to send their kids to the mosque and that they would even provide transportation. Many Bosnians responded positively and started sending their kids to the Turkish mosque. However, many Bosnians refugees did not want their kids to go to the mosque and learn about Islam. Many parents explained their choice to me, saying they did not want to force their kids to learn about any religion. Once they grew up, they wanted their kids to choose whatever religion they believed in. This especially was prevalent in interfaith marriages. Additionally, Bosnians are passionate about soccer, and thus have always been somewhat organized about pickup games and such. Above all however, Bosnian's take pride in their children's education, seeing it as an extension of their own success. Bosnians view education as the key to success in the new homeland for their children.

Throughout my work with Bosnians, I have been inspired by my own Muslim community. Listening to their stories about their journeys and observing their resilient natures made them even more remarkable in my eyes. They opened their hearts to me, eager to share their stories with the world. They wanted me to write about the challenge they faced and opportunities which befell them. Through these stories, they hope that their neighbors, employees, and their fellow Americans know more about them. They don't want to be these "others" any more.

Bosnian Muslims or Bosniaks, were always between two strong national movements from their neighbors, Serbia and Croatia. Bosnian Serbs consider Belgrade, the capital of Serbia, as their alternative home. The same is true for Bosnian Croats, who see Zagreb, the capital of Croatia, as their second home. Meanwhile, Bosnian Muslims don't have an alternative; Sarajevo is their only capital, and Bosnia and Herzegovina is their only home. No matter what the extent to which Bosnian Muslims practiced their faith, they always knew that the key to their very existence is a multi-religious and multi-cultural Bosnia. Therefore, they welcome and embraced religious and cultural diversity, a multi-ethnic Bosnia and Herzegovina. Nonetheless, they have been always seen, by both of their neighbors as the "others." Therefore, coming to the United States of America, the Bosnian community worked very hard to prove themselves as a decent addition to the American community.

Despite the common misconception that women in Islam don't have a place in the public society, I feel obligated to recognize women's contributions in organizing and establishing Bosnian Culture Center. For a few years, there was real female movement in the Bosnian Community. They initiated and successfully organized many community events.

I am extremely grateful to all those individuals who contributed and assisted me on this incredible journey to make this book a reality. Once again, I would especially like to thank two people who were an integral part of this work. First and foremost my dear professor Dr. Salahuddin Malik who assisted me until completion. He always made himself available to answer any questions or concerns. He guided me and taught me not only how to conduct good objective research, but also how to become a more rounded individual. It was my greatest pleasure to work and learn from Dr. Malik. Secondly, I would like to thank my dear friend Daniel Haug, whom I met, while working in customer support at Sutherland Global. Since then Daniel has become a good friend and adviser. He has helped me tremendously during the process of writing my research paper. He has become the friend of a lifetime.

xx

INTRODUCTION

INTRODUCTION

T his research is a first attempt to analytically study and discuss the Bosnian community of Rochester. As part of a larger study of the Muslim community in the Rochester metropolitan area, it is focused on the lives and experiences of a sample of 100 Bosnian families living in Rochester, most of whom have successfully integrated into a new environment, while facing many religious, cultural, and linguistic adjustments.

It is important to note that Bosnians are a unique component of the American melting pot. Bosnia and Herzegovina is a cross-cultural and cross-religious bridge, a unique place where the West and East blend. Bosnia is a place where the cultures of Rome, Charlemagne, the Ottomans, and the Austro-Hungarians overlapped.[1] It is truly a country unlike any other in Europe, where great imperial powers, faiths and cultures interacted with one another — an interaction which was usually hostile. Despite its small land mass, Bosnia and Herzegovina has permanently embedded its name into world history, paying its way with blood.

The earliest notable conflict occurred in 229 BC, during the battles between the largest world power at that time, the Roman Empire, and the indigenous Illyricum tribes known as Bellum Batonianum, who lived in the modern-day Bosnia and Herzegovina. The murder of Archduke France Ferdinand by a Serb nationalist in the capital of Bosnia and Herzegovina on June 28th, 1914 led to the outbreak of the First World War; this marking another bloody moment.[2] Most devastating and memorable, however, was the Bosnian genocide in April 1992, when Serbian forces systematically removed all Bosnian Muslims from Bosnia's cities bordering with Serbia.[3]

---

1. Neol Malcom, *Bosnia: A Short History. (Updated Edition, New York:* NYU Press, October 1, 1996).
2. Ibid., pg.155.
3. Norman Ciger, *Genocide in Bosnia: The Policy of Ethnic Cleansing* (Texas A&M University Press. June 1, 2000), pg. 3.

Subsequently, Bosnian Muslims were attacked using military equipment and human resources from former Yugoslavia.[4] Additionally, the genocidal massacre in the city of Srebrenica of over 8,000 Bosnians under the very eyes of a United Nations Dutch peacekeeping force made the Bosnian Muslims totally unsettled and insecure.[5] After this incident went public the floodgates of Bosnian emigration opened in the 21st century, when thousands of Bosnian immigrants opted to come to the United States and a several thousand, starting in 1993, settled in Rochester, New York.

This research describes how Bosnians were eager to assimilate into the American melting pot, but they desire to do so while preserving their faith and cultural traditions, thereby finding solace and comfort with each other.[6] Towards that end, they have already established a Bosnian Center for the socialization of community members. All of them have quickly adopted the new language for work place convenience. This work argues that Bosnian immigrants can maintain a desired level of confront in their adopted homeland while also retaining their cultural identity.[7] They hope that their offspring will become American without losing sight of who they were and from where they came.

While this research is intended to study and focus on the Bosnian community of Rochester, New York, it is also part of a the larger study encompassing the larger the greater Muslim community in the region. Because of the State Department sponsored Refugee Resettlement Program in Rochester, the Catholic Family Center facilitated the resettlement of refugees from all over the world. On September 17th, 1993, it opened its doors to the first wave of refugees from Yugoslavia.[8]

4. Salmedin Mesihović, *Rimski vuk i ilirska zmija. Posljednja borba* (Sarajevo: Nacionalna i univerzitetska biblioteka, 2011).
5. Lara J. Nettelfield & Sarah E. Wagnerm, *Srebrenica in the Aftermath of Genocide* (New York: Cambridge University Press, 2014).
6. The melting pot is a metaphor for a heterogeneous society becoming more homogeneous, the different elements "melting together" into a harmonious whole with a common culture. It is particularly used to describe the assimilation of immigrants in the United States. Source: United States. Bureau of the Census (1995*). Celebrating our nation's diversity: a teaching supplement for grades K-12. U.S. Dept. of Commerce, Economics and Statistics Administration, Bureau of the Census. pp. 1–. Retrieved on November 27, 2012.
7. Immigration is the movement of people into another country or region to which they are not native in order to settle there, especially as permanent residents or future citizens. Immigrants are motivated to leave their homeland for a variety of reasons, such as a desire for economic prosperity, political issues, family re-unification, escaping conflict or natural disaster, or simply the wish to change one's surroundings.
Source: "Definition of immigration by the Free Online Dictionary." Thefreedictionary.com. Retrieved on May 14, 2014.
8. Catholic Family Center's history goes back to 1917, when it was first known as Catholic Charities Aid Association of Rochester. In 1988, after decades of independent community service, the regional office merged with Catholic Youth Organization (CYO) and the Genesee Valley Office of Social Ministry, forming the multi-faceted human service agency now known as CFC. These organizations provide fam-

According to an unofficial Catholic Family Center report, there are approximately five thousand refugees from the former Yugoslavia living in the Greater Rochester area. The majority of these refugees, about 80%, are Bosnian Muslims from Bosnia and Herzegovina.[9] After twenty years of living here, Bosnians have inevitably been deeply affected by their host society. They have been influenced socially, culturally, economically, and politically.

According to the testimony of many Bosnian immigrants residing in Rochester, New York, as refugees and first generation to the city, they faced many difficulties. Some challenges included: language barrier, cultural differences, isolation, fear of being different and not accepted, fear of losing their ethnic and religious identity, prejudice, discrimination, and uncertainty of the future for their children. They also had to overcome inhumane treatment, deportation, grieving, trauma, revenge, forced labor, rape, destruction of cultural and religious monuments, illegal detention, starvation, loss of family members and more.

The majority of the participants in this research were Bosnian refugees having fled Bosnia as teenagers or young adults. As such, they were old enough to have formed personal connections to their home culture, religion and language, yet young enough to master and adapt to the systems of an American culture. This first generation must shoulder the burden of fostering solidarity, trust, cultural and religious appreciation among Bosnians in America while simultaneously having to prove their loyalty to their families and their home country. All of this while still facing personal challenges with their older parents, who live either in Bosnia or with them in Rochester. In addition, they face challenges with their own children, who have no memories of living in Bosnia and do not see their religion, language and culture through their parents' lens.

<hr>

ily strengthening programs, refugee resettlement, emergency housing and shelters, aging and adult programs, adoption and foster care, substance abuse treatment, behavioral health services and advocacy. Source: https://www.cfcrochester.org/about/history/retrieved June 2, 2016.
9. Feda Hadziosmanović, (Catholic Family Center Senior Job Developer), telephone interview, November 15, 2014.

The first group of twelve Bosnian refugees who came to Rochester was referred to The Islamic Center of Rochester on Westfall Road, where they found sympathetic company and their nominal heritage in Islam was revived. Here it is important to mention that the Islamic Center of Rochester played a pivotal role for the first Bosnian refugees along with the Catholic Family Center and the Turkish community in Rochester.[10]

---

10. The first group of Bosnians who arrived in Rochester later on provided significant help and guidance to subsequent Bosnian arrivals in Rochester.

THE FIRST TWELVE BOSNIAN REFUGEES ARRIVING TO ROCHESTER

The first wave of Bosnian refugees, a group of twelve, arrived in Rochester on September 17th, 1993. The Spahić Family was among the first to arrive: father Husein, mother Enisa, and son Amel. Then, Esad Tutundzić with his wife Mirsada and daughter Elma were added to this group. In the same group the following members also came: Hasan Malkić, who arrived the night before, Hasan Dzananović, Edin Aziri, and Gorana Sefo with two small children. Amel Spahić remembers very well the day when he arrived in Rochester, NY and remembers challenges they faced in Rochester and the United States of America. It is pertinent to provide the lengthy and detailed observations of the first generations refugee family in Rochester, which will help to understand their state of mind even in such a friendly city Rochester.

> Four hundred Bosnian refugees left Vienna, Austria and landed in New York on September 17th, 1993 where the people from International Organization for Migration (IOM) waited for us.[11] We had a hard time communicating, but we understood that we would be separated and sent to different cities. IOM people started to call us, but it was very hard to communicate with them since they did not pronounce our names correctly. There were twelve people called to go to Rochester, NY and among them were my father Hussein, my mom Enis, Esad Tutandzic and his wife Mirsada. They also had a young daughter Elma.

11. Established in 1951, International Organization for Migration (IOM) is the leading inter-governmental organization in the field of migration and works closely with governmental, intergovernmental and non-governmental partners. With 162 member states, a further 9 states holding observer status and offices in over 100 countries, IOM is dedicated to promoting humane and orderly migration for the benefit of all. It does so by providing services and advice to governments and migrants. Source: http://www.iom.int/about-iom, retrieved on June 15, 2016.

There was another woman Gordana Sefo with two small children too. Also in our group were various single men: Hasan Malkić, Hasan Dzananovic, Edin Aziri.

The people from the IOM took us to the terminal for Rochester and made sure we boarded the airplane. On the way to Rochester, there were issues with the airplane and we had to do an emergency landing in Utica. They enlisted some taxicabs and sent us to the Rochester airport where our sponsors were waiting for us, accompanied by translators Nina Ibrahimovic, Zvonko Matana, and Lena Horwath. Our sponsors were from the Islamic Center of Rochester and Turkish Islamic Center. From the airport, they took us to the Islamic Center of Rochester where many people, Pakistani and Turks, were waiting for us with a lot of food and presents. After dinner, they started deciding who would take whom.

Turkish Imam Mehmet Aktas with his wife Nuran took my family in, and we went to his house. It was a very beautiful house, and they were extremely nice and considerate. We stayed with Imam Mehmet's family for some time, until they found an apartment for us. They gave us furniture, food, everything we needed. Other Turkish families helped us. Now we had everything needed, but we were not happy because my sister was still in Croatia with her husband and son. My mother cried every day; she prayed very hard that my sister, Amela, with her family, would join us. We started going to school to learn English. Still many Turkish families would come and drop off food, or other items. Life was getting better. After three months, my sister, with her family, finally came to Rochester. We were all happy, especially my mom. She started laughing again and making the best Bosnian food, and my mother made it better than did anyone else. She was always drinking coffee and making Bosnian food. We were plan-ning to stay in America just until the war was over, but we are still here. Tragically both of my parents passed away. Losing them both was very hard for me, but I still have my sister and her family. In addition, living in Rochester for twenty-one years makes it my home. I love this city and I am planning to live here until my time comes.[12]

---

12 Amel Spahić, e-mail message to author, November 20th, 2014.

Figure I.1. Amel Spahić with his mother Enisa Spahić.

CHAPTER ONE

RESEARCH BACKGROUND

The focus of this book is to tell the story of Bosnian Muslim refugees living in Rochester, New York, while providing a brief overview of the history of Bosnia and Herzegovina and other Bosnian immigrantsin the United States of America, particularly Muslim Bosnian refugees. This research is the result of extensive interviews with Bosnian refugees, written surveys, observations of the Bosnian community at the Bosnian mosque currently located at 312 Fisher Road, Rochester, NY, and personal engagements. This project study is the first of its kind in this region and is of historical importance. Despite their economic well-being, this group faces many challenges, including religious, cultural, language, and identity crises, especially among the American-born younger generation. In particular, this study will address pressing issues in the Bosnian community, including dealing with trauma, alcohol and drug abuse, increased divorce rates, and arguments within the Bosnian community, specifically between secular and practicing Muslims. In addition, this research intends to provide an understanding of the experiences and lives of Bosnian Muslim families prior to the war, the experiences and disruptions of the war, and their present lives in the United States. This research analyzes the struggles they faced in coming to a new country.

The Bosnian community in the United States is small, but it does have historical significance because of its distinctive European roots and its Islamic heritage. It is important to understand that Bosnia and Herzegovina was part of the Ottoman Empire for 400 years. During this time, the majority of its population embraced and practiced Islam and was exposed to the Islamic religion and culture as well as the Turkish and Arabic languages.

Turkish was an administrative language while Arabic was learned for re-ligious purposes. Meanwhile, parallel to these two languages, Bosnians also used their native Bosnian language. After 400 years living under the Ottoman Empire, in 1878, Bosnia and Herzegovina was incorporated into Austro-Hungary. The new empire sharply changed the lives Bosnians had grown accustomed too, forcing Bosnians towards Christian Europe and its religion, culture, and language.

During the meeting of the Anti-Fascist Council of Bosnia – Herzegovina on November 25th, 1943 in Mrkonić-grad, the Socialist Republic of Bosnia and Herzegovina was formed as a political and independent entity and be-came the predecessor of the modern-day Bosnia and Herzegovina, one of the six constituent federal units forming the former Yugoslavia. Now November 25th is celebrated as Statehood day of Bosnia and Herzegovina. Because of its complex religious makeup of Islam, Orthodox Christianity and Roman Catholics, in addition to the Slavic language, the Slovenian writer Josip Vidmar rightly described Bosnia's history as "the most complicated country in Europe."[13] Therefore, if we neglect to collect, record, and preserve the sto-ries and memories from first-generation Bosnians who lived in two different political ideologies and philosophies — the Communist and Democratic re-gimes, in Bosnia and the United States respectively — their stories, experi-ences, observations and insights into the two distinct regimes, will be lost.

---

13. Lovrenović, ibid., pg, 109.

RESEARCH PAPER SAMPLE SELECTION

This research project is focused on the lives and experiences of a sample of 100 Bosnian families living in Rochester who have successfully adapted to their new environment, but who are still struggling with emotional backlash from the war. This is an oral history project with the primary objective of recording testimonies from Bosnian refugees, including the sometime incomprehensibly tragic experiences. These stories include Bosnian children whose fathers were taken from them and killed because of their faith. These children had to leave their safety net: home, schools, friends, environment neighborhood. As they left behind all they ever knew, they were forced to go to a new and strange world. One of these is Senada Smajić, now aged 24. In her email, she wrote the following: "My name is Senada Smajić and I am 24 years old. I came to the United States in February 1999 at the age of nine. I came here not knowing a bit of English. I felt like I did not belong here, I missed home so much."

Another Bosnian, Hilmo Kapić, came to Rochester, NY in March 1994 when he was sixteen years old. In an e-mail, he described sentiments of loss and homesickness: "I lost everything in the war, my house was burned down. I took a bus from Zagreb to Vienna, Austria. From Vienna, I flew to JFK International Airport where I arrived with just some clothing in my backpack. We stayed overnight in New York City. The following day we came to Rochester by American Airlines. In the beginning, I did not like living in the city where there was too much crime and it was very unsafe. I wanted to go back home but there was no home to go back to." Similarly, Fatima Razić, now a 35-year-old singer-songwriter in Rochester, came to America when she was sixteen years old.

Figure 1.1. Fatima Razić - Singer-songwriter.

She first came to Saint Louis, but eventually settled in Rochester where she graduated high school and attended the Rochester Institute of Technology (RIT). She earned her Bachelors and later Masters in Information Technology from RIT. In an interview she gave to the local city newspaper, she said, "I grew up in Bosnia. The war started when I was 10. My sister and I fled the city and were jumping on the buses trying to get out. At one point we got separated. We went to Croatia for three and a half years. My parents stayed back because they wanted to protect everything they'd built their whole life."[14] Her parents were sent to the concentration camps because of their faith. Fatima did not see her parents for a long time and her first song "When Will I See You Again" was dedicated to her father. The lyrics came directly from the letter she wrote to her father when she was 10 years old.[15]

In addition, there are stories of working men and women who worked their entire life to build their homes and families, yet had to leave everything behind. Esma Aganović, a Bosnian woman, lived twenty-nine years in her beautiful village Bešnjevo, near the city of Šipovo where the political configuration was 82% Serbs and 12% Muslims. In 1992, all 12% of Muslims were forced to leave their homes, fleeing to neighboring city Jajce to save their lives. "It was hard." Esma recalls, "to leave my home behind. I worked very hard and built a house for many years, and bought furniture piece by piece. I loved and cherished everything I accomplished in my life, and suddenly I was forced to leave my home and my work, and everything I built with my own hard work.

14. Frank De Blasé. "Fatima Razic builds beauty out of an ugly world." Source:http://www.rochestercitynewspaper.com/rochester/fatima-razic-builds-beauty-out-of-anuglyorld/Content?oid=2693448CITY_newsletter_121615&utm_medium=email&utm_term=0_53671db549-b54627c313-297659133
15. Ibid.

It was hard and painful. I had to leave with my small son and old, sick mother. I lived in a refugee center in Zenica for seven years with my son and mother."[16]

In addition, there are other tragic stories of Bosnian widows who were left to care for their children alone after their husbands were killed. Fatima Salkanović is one such widow, whose husband was killed by Serbs in 1995 while defending his country. Fatima at the time was only twenty-four years old and her two small children were four and one year old. After her husband's death, she lived with her children in Bosnia for six years, but it was extremely hard to survive in Bosnia without income and with two small children. Eventually, she heard that the United States was accepting widows and children from Bosnia, so she applied and she was accepted to proceed to her new homeland. She came to Rochester in 2001 with her two sons. Her older son Aldin was ten and her younger son Elmedin was seven years old. Fatima recalls the time when she first came to Rochester, New York.

> I came to Rochester in 2001 with two small kids. I felt alone and lost. It wasn't easy to come to a foreign country with two kids. I did not have relatives in Rochester to help me out. I did, however, have a few friends who made my transition easier. Nevertheless, my friends could not help me much because they were not in any position to do so. They also were newcomers and had a lot of issues on their plate. At first, it was painful, but I was patient and determined to succeed since there was not a way back to Bosnia where I had struggled for six years with my sons.[17]

There are other stories of Bosnian mothers whose sons were taken from them and whose remains have never been found. One of these Bosnian mothers is Sadika Kolobodanović, an eighty-four-year-old Bosnian woman, whose son was killed by Bosnian Serbs in Doboj, a city in Bosnia and Herzegovina. Sadika, like many other Bosnians, never found out what happened to her son.

16. Esma Aganović, personal interview with author, November 28, 2014.
17. Fatima Salkanović, facebook message to author, October 10, 2016.

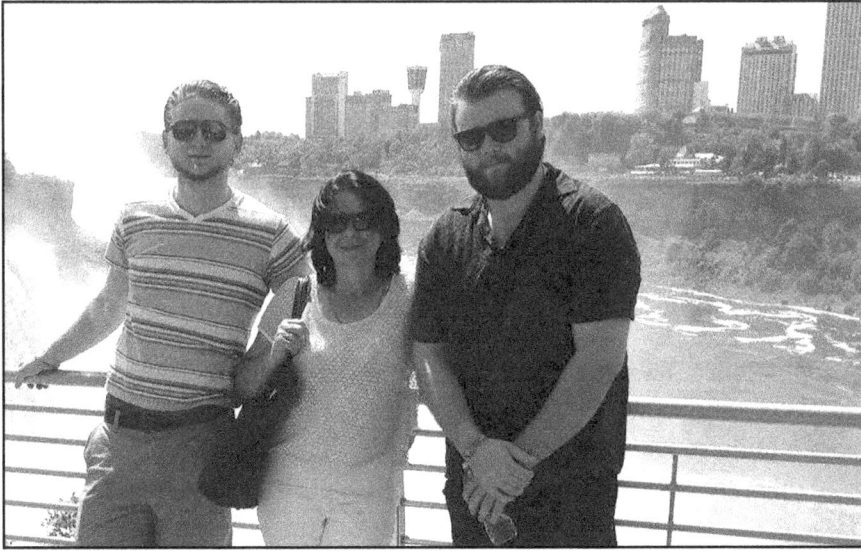

Figure 1.2. Fatima Salkanović with her two sons visiting Niagara Falls, August 2015.

Twenty years later, she is still searching and hoping that the remains of her son will finally be found. Sadika is restless; even though she has two sons and grandchildren living in Rochester, she cannot find peace because of her loss. Before coming to Rochester, Sadika lived and worked in Germany. One night, Sadika recalls coming home from work at a time when she felt lost and mentally exhausted with her new life in Germany. Overwhelmed with the war in Bosnia and not knowing where her son was, Sadika sat down and started writing a poem about her missing son, Ago. She wrote to release her pain and share it with the world, hoping that someone would listen to her cry in verse and call her with information about her son. While crying she said loudly, "My God, where is my son Ago. What happened to him?" She wrote the following poem:

> Volim Doboj volim okolinu u Doboju lijepu Gradinu. Svuda idem svuda   tražim, o Gradino ti mi kaži, gdje je moje milo zlato, ostalo je meni nepoznato. Svake noći u samoći, čekam kad ćeš sine Agiću doći. Ja u Dojču suze lijem, Bosno kaži gdje mi sina kriješ. Svuda idem svuda tražim, o Gradino ti mi kaži, Gdje je moje milo zlato, ostalo je meni nepoznato."[18]

18. Sadika Kolobodanović, personal interview with author, August 14th, 2015.

Loosely translated, it reads:

I like Doboj: the neighboring towns of Doboj: a beautiful fortress. Everywhere I go, everywhere I search, oh fortress you tell me, where is my dear boy, he is lost to me. Every night when I'm alone I wait for when my son Agić will return. In Germany I cry: Bosnia tell me wheremy son is. Everywhere I go, everywhere I search, oh for tress you tell me, where is my dear boy, he is lost to me."

Soon after, Sadika appeared on one of the Bosnian radio stations in Germany and recited her poem during her interview, asking listeners for help to find her son Ago. Shortly afterwards, she received hundreds of calls from other Bosnian grieving mothers, whose sons were killed and some still missing. She concludes, "Even though they did not help me find my son, I still felt better knowing that I am not the only mother whose son's remains where not found. I also hoped that government would look for our sons' remains since there were many Bosnians' sons still missing and their relatives were searching for their remains."[19] Unfortunately, even to this day, her son Ago is still missing. He was killed by his Serb nationalist neighbors because of his identity and religion. Sadika, an eighty-four-year-old Bosnian woman, still has only one wish, as she said during our interview: "Before I die I want to find my son's remains so I can bury him properly."[20] Sadika cried during our entire interview.

Figure: 1.3. Sadika Kolobodanović.

19. Ibid.
20. Ibid.

Although her son Ago was killed so long ago, it was still heartbreaking to listen to this pained mother talking about her missing son.

There are stories about women, like Dževahira Hamzić, who had to go from country to country, until finally settling in Rochester, NY and finding a new home. She left her mother, two sisters, and two nephews in Pakistan and came to America with her father. Dževahira will never forget the moment she heard, along with her neighbors, that they should leave the city immediately because of Četniks.[21] These were Serbian nationalist fighters and a division of the Serbian army during the Bosnian war and, were entering the city. They went to Bugojno, a neighboring city which was, however, constantly under heavy fire. Dževahira's sister said that she had a friend who lived in Split, Croatia and she suggested they should all travel there. Dževahira's whole family decided to go to Croatia and they stayed with her for a month. Her family was big and the apartment small, so they decided to go to another city, Makarska, Promajna, where they had often stayed for summer vacations. They called another friend and asked if she had empty room for them. Her friend allowed them to stay there for two years. Unfortunately, the Četniks were traveling in that direction, towards Promajna. "At that moment, we really did not know where to go," said Dževahira.

Sedžida Siladžić, who at the time was a Bosnian Ambassador to Pakistan, said that she would take Dževahira and her family to Pakistan. Everything was happening so fast and they simply had to flee to Pakistan. They were placed in Rawalpindi, in a *Hajji* camp, a refugee camp for two years. After two years they had the choice of going either to Australia, Canada or America. Because she already had a cousin who lived in America, they decided to relocate there. However, at the last minute, her cousin told them that she could not be their sponsor because her brother was coming from Bosnia and she could not receive both parties. Luckily, other families who were in the camp helped them find a sponsor. When they arrived in Rochester in 1995, there were around 150 people from Bosnia already there.

---

21 John F. Burns, "150 Muslims Say Serbs Raped Them in Bosnia"
"Accusations of widespread rape by the Serbian fighters began circulating in April and May, soon after the conflict began, when irregular paramilitary groups known as Chetniks, some from Serbia and others from Bosnia, swept through predominantly Muslim areas of eastern Bosnia. Patterns of Brutality"
Source: http://www.nytimes.com/1992/10/03/world/150-muslims-say-serbs-raped-them-in-bosnia.html.
Retrieved: January 23, 2017.

The atmosphere amongst the first Bosnian refugee was great; they were close because of their shared experience of the war in Bosnia, the hardship encountered, and the time spent in Pakistan. There was a drastic change between Pakistan and America. Pakistan was a very poor country with different culture, food, and clothing, but in America, they felt much better. They started to go to school and learn English. Through school, doctors' appointments, administrative and social services they met other Bosnian families. Dževahira continues:

> Everybody was nice to one another and they respected each other. Unfortunately, now it is much different. One of the Bosnian refugees who came before me, she took me and other Bosnian women to the mosque. However, she took us to the Ahmadiyya Mosque located on 1609 E Main St, Rochester, NY. Before that, I did not know anything about the Ahmadiyya sect. One of the women, called Ruffi, who was sponsoring one of the Bosnian families, gave us a small book titled "Truth about Ahmadiyya" about Ahmadiyya beliefs translated into Bosnian so we could know what kind of mosque this was. Miss Ruffi helped numerous Bosnian women, including myself. Months later, we learned about the Turkish mosque and we started to go there. They received us with open hands. They were very kind and generous towards us.

Figure 1.4. Dževahira Hamzić.

I am so happy that we now have our own place, our own mosque, but I still feel very sad that we left the Turks. I truly loved going to the Turkish mosque and it felt like home. It was enough space for everybody, especially when they bought the addition where the Bosnian women used to gather. I simply can't get over it. Even to this day, I ask why we had to go from the Turkish mosque.[22]

There are heartbreaking stories about parents who did everything in their power to bring their children out of the warzone and poverty to a safer place, just to sadly lose their kids in America to bad marriages or alcohol/drug abuse, or both. Even though interfaith marriages were not strange to Bosnian Muslims, Remza Hadžić and her husband did not expect that they would have to deal with this challenge when they left Bosnia and Herzegovina in 2000 and came to America, Rochester, NY. Remza's journey from Bosnia to America was anything but easy. In 1992, while her husband was fighting in the Bosnian Army she escaped her home, a beautiful village called Ševarlije near city of Doboj. While pregnant with her son, she along with her daughter Šejla, her mother in law and two sisters in law, left for Croatia. In her village, in one day Četniks killed over fifty civilians, including Remza's father-in-law. After six years, they managed to find their remains and did fifty salāt al-Janāzah, or the Islamic funeral prayer, for Bosnian Muslims who were killed by their neighbors. It was a devastating time for her family.

After two years, her husband managed to visit them in Croatia and brought them back to Zenica, a city under Bosnian Army control, where he found an apartment for Remza, their children and his mother. Unfortunately, they could not go back to their home since Serbian nationalist had occupied Doboj, including her village. In Zenica, Remza managed to find a job working for a project called Empatija that was founded and financed by the Netherlands where women of Bosnia would bring their children to kindergarten and elementary school while the mothers would crochet and sew. That program went well for her since she was able to make some money and her husband could visit her frequently. Unfortunately, the project was short-lived.

---

22. Dževahira Hamzić, personal interview with author, August 15, 2014.

After two and half years, the Bosnian Army discharged her husband and anyone else over the age of 35, since the war was officially over. As a means of compensating damage to property, the government offered around 20,000 marks in materials for building houses or fixing land for farming. However, because their village, along with their land, was still under Serbian control, they were not able to do anything with this compensation. Instead, they applied to come to America, because her brother was married and lived there already. Eventually, they were accepted to travel to America on September 29th, 2000. When they arrived in Rochester, NY, her daughter Šejla was seventeen. Despite her age, she quickly learned English and was able to drop her accent. Remza did not go to school to learn English because she started working instead; she learned English with her son, Mirza. Every day, after work, she would listen to tapes and read with him. She started working on December 1st, 2000 and December 1st, 2016 marks her sixteenth anniversary working at the same company.

After six years, Remza managed to buy a house. Meanwhile, her daughter Šejla finished high school and two years of Community College. After a few years, she started working and met an American man, Russell Herbert, whom she wanted to marry. Her parents were strongly opposed, especially Šejla's father. He said despite religious and cultural differences, something about that man bothered him from day one. However, despite her fathers' strong objection, Šejla was in love with Russell and moved to Montana, far away from her family. They got married and Remza went to Montana to see her daughter. Meanwhile, Šjela found a job but Russell did not work. Neither Remza nor her husband was happy about their daughter working while her husband sat at home. After a year without working, Russell joined Šjela at a customer support agency, where they eventually worked different shifts to raise their newborn daughter. Soon, Šejla found a job in a bank after passing an exam as a loan officer. She started making more money, so her husband quit his job. In this time, he started an extra-marital affair with their daughter's kindergarten teacher. Šejla told her mother about the affair and told her that she would love to get divorced but Russell refused to give up their children and she could not leave them. Soon, Russell started to go to school and began another affair. Meanwhile Šejla asked her parents for financial help and they started giving her $500 each month to pay the mortgage and bills. After six months, they told her that she should sell her house and find an apartment for her and her children, so she did. They sold the house and split the money, choosing to live separately.

Šejla continued to live in Missoula with her two kids and Russell moved to Kalispell, where he attended college and lived with his new girlfriend. According to Šejla's friend, Russell had started drinking and abusing drugs, which was why Šejla had asked for financial help. Moreover, she believes, he suffered from Post-Traumatic Stress Disorder. One day, he came home very drunk and while Šejla was cleaning the garage, he was bothering her and provoking her. They started fighting and she pushed him. He called police and she ended up spending a night in a prison, while her children were taken away from her. She spent few days with her friend because he did not allow her to come back home. Soon after this incident they separated and he moved to Kalispell, taking their children with him. Šejla went to Kalispell to see her children, and when she confronted Russell, she lost her life. Here is how Remza describes this devastating and tragic event:

> It was Friday, March 13th, 2015. We came from work and my husband and I went to the grocery store. We came back, did some housework and went to sleep. We both left our phones in the living room. It was midnight when we heard the phone ringing, again and again. My husband went to the kitchen and answered the phone. It was the police from Montana calling to inform us that there had been a confrontation between Šejla and her husband, and that Šejla was dead. They didn't know the details, but it appeared that Šejla died from a self-inflicted gunshot wound to the head. They called us three times, each time with different story about the event. Eventually they said that my daughter killed herself while fighting with her husband over the gun.[23]

23. Dennis Brag, "Woman died of self-inflicted gunshot during struggle over gun" MTN News. Mar 14,

We called and informed my brother and he immediately came over with other friends. They start looking for airplane tickets for my husband and I, but my brother said,' no, Remza don't go, I will go. They went to Kalispell, Montana, where they were treated by the police very poorly; they said the police were unprofessional, showing no empathy, treating them like second class citizens. But I didn't believe it. I felt that something else happened, but we didn't have money to pay for a private investigation. Now my daughter is dead. Her two kids are without a mother, and he is a free man. We wanted the body of our daughter to be brought to Rochester, close to us, but because she was not divorced, even though the divorce was in process, they had to wait for her husband's signature.

My husband and my brother stayed in Montana for five days, waiting for an autopsy and for the signature from her husband. While waiting for the body to be released, they wanted to see her kids, but that did not go well. Finally, one of the police officers felt sorry and organized for the kids to meet their grandpa and grand uncle. Šejla's friend brought the kids to meet their grandpa in a pizzeria. Do you know what is most tragic in all this? I left my home in Bosnia after Četniks killed my neighbors, including my father-in-law, to save the lives of my kids. I came to the United States with my kids to provide them with better opportunities, so they could finish school and go to college. It was very hard in the beginning. We had to work long hours in order to save enough money to buy our first car to ease our commute to work. We are a hard-working family, honest and well-respected. After six years in Rochester, we bought our house. In the last few years, we also repaired our home in Bosnia. I lost my daughter here in the United States, where she should have been safe and protected. I lost my daughter! How do you process that! My daughter was taken from me.

2015 3:55. Source:http://www.krtv.com/story/28510028/woman-died-of-self-inflicted-gunshot-during-struggle-over-gun. Retrieved: December 26, 2016. Related video: https://www.youtube.com/watch?v=-gIUAaB5u-Xk

My daughter was a hard-working woman and, she managed to get a job as a loan officer. Even if they say something happened to her, he made her that way. She was by herself, working most of the time alone to support their two kids and him. He was abusing alcohol and drugs and my daughter was to embarrassed to tell us about this. Now we go to visit our grandkids and we send them presents and we have to maintain an acceptable relationship with Russell if we want a relationship with our grandkids, but I am sure that the truth will come out one day. What also hurt me to the core was when my grandkids talked about his current wife, they called her 'mom'. I simply couldn't believe that. I told Ena, my granddaughter, that she is not your mom, do you know who your mom is, your mom is Šejla and she is dead, not that woman.

One day you have to find out what happened to your mom. His whole family never called us, not once. What kind of family is that? I do not want to say anything bad because of my grandkids. I love them so much and I do not want to hurt them in any way. I agreed to this interview because I want everyone to know what happened to my daughter.

Figure 1.5. Remza Hadžić with her daughter Šejla and granddaughter Ena and grandson Carson.

Figure 1.6 Šejla's Hadžić Herbert grave in Rochester, NY.

I want Americans to know what hard-working and decent people we are. Also, when my grandkids grow up, I want to talk to them about my daughter, their mom. I want to tell them all of the facts and they can make their own judgement. Also, my Šejla grew up always moving, from Croatia to Zenica, then America, always a new school and new cultural environment. Constantly, we were fighting for our basic needs and survival: paying rent and buying enough food to survive. When we came to America, she went to school during the day and at night would help us clean a school, to buy our first car. Then she fell in love and went from home. I cried and cried.

Perhaps the best example is that of a historical woman figure whose fate best mirrors so many straggles by Bosnian women throughout history is Queen Catherine, known incorrectly as "the last Bosnian queen," who is without a doubt one of the most interesting personalities of the Bosnian Dynasty. It is a misfortune that Katarina was not actually the last queen, because her life mirrors so many of Bosnian women who had to leave their beloved country to save their own and their children's lives. Like many other Bosnian women, after the Ottoman Empire occupation in 1463, she moved to the Republic of Dubrovnik where she acted as the legal representative of the Bosnian kingdom. Hoping, as many Bosnian refugees who had to leave their country, that her kingdom would quickly be liberated. But, as time passed, and liberation became unlikely, she moved to Rome in 1466 where she lived out her days never seeing her children again, passing away in 1479.[24] So many Bosnian women shared this fate. Their sons were taken from them and killed; their fathers, brothers, and husbands were also killed as they were forced to leave their country, many of whom never managed to return to see their children, fathers or brothers again.[25]

24. Bazilije Pandzić, *Bosanska Kraljica Katarina* (Hrvatski Kalendar, 1978), pp. 179-184.
25. William S. Walker. *German and Bosnian Voices In A Time Of Crisis: Bosnian Refugees in Germany 1992-2002* (Indianapolis, IN: Dog Ear Publishing, LLC.2012).

RESEARCH PAPER FRAMEWORK

This work briefly discusses the rich history of Bosnian immigrants in the United States of America, with its focus on Bosnian settlers in the Rochester Area. The paper argues for Bosnian immigrants, retaining their religious, ethnic and cultural identity through organizing themselves via religious and cultural organizations. This so that they can continue practicing their traditions while trying to avoid creating a wall of separation between their new homeland and themselves. Furthermore as the Bosnian community needs to integrate, but not assimilate, in the American melting pot. Additionally, this paper argues that a majority of Bosnian refugees in the United States, primarily the first-generation immigrants, have become victims of inner conflict between retaining their old culture versus the new American culture. The aim of this research is to provide an analytical insight into the challenges facing Bosnian Muslims and suggest solutions to these challenges.

RESEARCH PAPER METHOD

This research study is based on thirty-five surveys, thirty taped interviews, fifteen written interviews, twenty phone interviews, and the author's extensive personal knowledge of the Bosnian community of Rochester, having worked with them for over fifteen years. Respondents participating in this research come from various socio-economic and religious backgrounds covering a variety of occupations. Mostly, participants in this research take active interest in community affairs. Interviews were scheduled via personal contacts, phone, email or Facebook.

Obtaining interviews from so many Bosnians was a challenging task even for a Bosnian who has worked closely within the Bosnian community for fifteen years.

Bosnian community members were very suspicious and reserved when asked for interviews. Many of them were afraid to give an interview for a variety of reasons. Some simply did not want to have their name mentioned, as they said "for security reasons." Some participants did not want to disclose their identity because their stories or life choices did not align with Bosnian standards or traditions. Others did not want to express their "honest" views; therefore, they refused to give an official interview, but they were very generous in sharing their insights off the record. Many questioned the importance, purpose and goal of these interviews. Finally, after detailed explanations on the purpose of this research, I managed to persuade them that I was only interested in their stories because they have historical significance and that our stories and experiences matter for future generations.

On the other hand, there were Bosnians who were eager to share their stories and war experiences with me, offering their time for an interview even without my asking. As time progressed, towards the end of the research, many Bosnians offered their stories, insights, observations, fears, their moments of extreme happiness or sadness, their struggles, and their successes.

INTERVIEW SUMMARY SHOWING CHALLENGES FACED BY BOSNIAN REFUGEES

Even though a majority of Bosnian refugees initially agreed to an interview, some of them never responded to interview requests. Some immediately declined, while others originally agreed, but had to cancel at the last minute. In a few instances, a person agreed and gave an interview but requested not to publish the names or anything we discussed, which I found an odd request. Similarly, many were happy to share their stories, but wanted to stay anonymous. As stated above, many Bosnians were reluctant to open up or give an interview at the beginning of the research, but as time passed, some of them would approach or call me and offer to be part of the research and share their experiences. Some were especially interested if their picture could be published along with the interview. Occasionally, even after the interview was finished, they offered to write more about their personal experiences in Bosnia during the war and their journey to America. One participant told me that he has written memoirs about his life and struggles during the war, but he could not give it to me, because he hopes that one day his children will publish it. However, he did offer me an extensive, long interview. Surveys were performed personally during in-home visits or at the Bosnian mosque, Bosnia & Herzegovina Culture Center of Rochester, located at 312 Fisher Rd, Rochester, NY. Other interviews were completed in local coffee shops or over the phone. Usually the interviews were done in Bosnian and on a one-to-one basis, except in a few instances where both a husband and wife wanted to share their stories.

The majority of Bosnians interviewed were very generous in sharing their stories and their journey, often indirect, from Bosnia to America. Proudly, they would talk about their lives prior to the war and share pictures of their homes and families. Usually they would tell a story or two from that time, when their whole family was together, referring to that time as "the good old days." When talking about Bosnia before the war, their faces were happy, eyes shiny and voices excited. As soon as they started talking about their lives during the war, their faces would turn sad, eyes would be full of tears and all the excitement left their voices. Usually they needed a few moments to collect themselves before they could go on. These stories focused on family members who were killed during the war. It is hard to find a single Bosnian family who did not lose somebody in the war. Occasionally, as in the case of Eniz Kurspahić, whose family was burned alive, some did not want to discuss the details of the tragedy during the official interview but they opened up afterwards. Eniz briefly talked to me about his family, especially his young and beautiful daughter who died before the war. His daughter was tall and had long hair. She was full of life and loved playing basketball. Eniz talked about his young daughter for a while, looking in the empty space trying to capture her image. Even before the war, Eniz had lost one of his daughters. His two other daughters, his mother, and his wife were burned alive. Here is how Eniz started and finished his interview with me:

> My name is Eniz Kurspahić and I came to the United States of America, to the city of Rochester, in 1996. My family was burned alive in a village near Višegrad, a city in Bosnia. My mother, my wife, and my two daughters were burned alive by our Serbian neighbors and Serbs from Serbia. When we heard that Serbs were coming to our village, our elders told us that men and boys should leave the village immediately and try to reach the safety zone. If we stayed they would kill all of the men. We did not have any weapons to defend ourselves. We knew they would kill all men and boys, but we hoped they wouldn't kill women and children. We hoped their lives would be spared, because the international community was watching. The world was watching and they wouldn't kill women and children, but they locked them in my house: my mother, my wife, my two daughters, and lit the house on fire.

They burned them alive, and all of my family was incinerated. Only Jasmin my son lived. I went to Srebrenica, to the safe zone, with my son, Jasmin who was at the time 15 years old. I was captured by Serbs on August 17, 1995, transported to Žepa, and from there went to a concentration camp in Serbia. Eventually, with the help of UNICEF, together with my son Jasmin I came to America.[26]

During our official interview he did not want to talk much. He handed me a piece of paper, a copied newspaper article which contained an interview that he and his son Jasmin gave to Christine Van Susan, a *Democrat and Chronicle* reporter, about their life in Bosnia, the loss of their family, their life in Rochester and their masonry business. Eniz told Van Susan, "I was very happy with the life we had before the war. I never planned or imagined leaving that life, but I like it here as well."[27] Eniz with his son Jasmin opened a masonry business here in Rochester and built many beautiful stone walls. Unfortunately, Eniz can no longer work due to illness. A year ago, Eniz was diagnosed with lung cancer. On September 1st, 2016 I asked him if he would sit down with me and talk a little bit more about his life in Rochester agin, but he declined. He just said "I simply want to be alone."[28] Most women were more open and willing to talk about their lives in Bosnia during the war; they would also talk about their husbands' struggles as well. In these cases, the man would usually listen silently to his wife's rendition.

Dzevahira Hamzić, a Bosnian woman who has been living with Eniz for 15 years, talked about her struggle living with Eniz whose family was burned alive. She said that he was drinking alcohol instead of water and was smoking constantly, cigarette after cigarette. "The only time he did not either drink or smoke was when he was sleeping, which he rarely did. In the middle of night, he would wake up, scream, and cry, especially at the beginning of our relationship. I truly believe that if I was not living with him, he would not stay in his right mind. I do not think he would have survived. I was his nurse; I was his psychiatrist, his doctor."[29]

---

26. Eniz Kurspahić, personal interview with author, September 1, 2016.
27. Kurspahić, ibid.
28. Ibid.
29. Hamzić, ibid.

Interviews usually lasted about 30 to 50 minutes. However, off the record, interviewees would share many more stories about their lives and struggles during the wartime in Bosnia, as well as current challenges they are facing in America. Bosnians who have retired would love to live in Bosnia, but since their children are here, they have to stay here to be close to them. Moving to Bosnia would mean leaving their children and grandchildren thousands of miles away. However, in Bosnia, they would be more self-sufficient, not to mention that they would be back in their homes. Rafija Kapić, a 64-year-old Bosnian refugee, who was among the first group who came to Rochester from Bosnia, said, "Next year I will go to Bosnia and spend some time there. I miss my family, my sisters, my neighbors; I miss everyone and everything in Bosnia. I simply cannot wait to go. I just miss them."[30]

Many older Bosnians save up money to visit Bosnia usually every two years. However, some never went back. Kadria Fazlic, a 72-year-old Bosnian woman, came to America before the war erupted, in 1980. She works as a translator for Bosnian refugees residing in Rochester, especially refugees over 50 years old. She never visited Bosnia and Herzegovina, but she would love to go with her older daughter, who also has never been there to visit. Kadria said, "I would like to go to Sarajevo, my birth place, with my daughter Aysha. I would love to go and see my city and visit the streets and places where I grew up. I also would love my daughter to see our house, our relatives. Aysha promised me that she would take me next year. I hope I will be in good health."[31]

Some of the participants are concerned about their older parents who still live in Bosnia and did not want to join them. This separation produces feelings of guilt and internal conflict because they left them behind. Many invited their parents to come to America and live with them for a few months. One of them is Minka Bibic, who has a sister and brother living near her in her neighborhood in Rochester. She invites her mother to come from Bosnia to visit her and her siblings.

---

30. Refija Kapić, personal interview with author, September 1, 2016.
31. Fatima Fazlić, personal Interview with author, September 1, 2016.

Her mother usually stays with them for a few months. However, despite her love for their children and grandchildren, she still prefers to live in Bosnia because of her children's busy schedules and work obligations. Minka said:

> I would love for my mom to stay and live here with me or my sister or brother, wherever she prefers, but she doesn't want to because we all work the whole day and she would be alone. She does not drive and she has to stay at home the whole day by herself, until we come back. On the other hand, in Bosnia she can walk and meet and socialize with her friends and relatives. She doesn't depend on anybody. I know it is better for her in Bosnia but she is getting older and I worry about her. I feel guilty that she is living alone now after my father passed away. But I understand her, financially, she doesn't depend on us, her children, because my father left a good pension and she is happier in Bosnia. Once I retire, I also plan to go to Bosnia.[32]

Figure 1.7. From the left, Minka Bibić, with her sister Nurzata Đokić, her mother, Ema Vrbanjac during her visit to the United States, city of Rochester and her brother Nedžad Vrbanjac.

---

32. Minka Bibić, personal interview with author, November 11, 2014.

Unlike Minka and her siblings, whose mother is financially secure, the majority of Bosnian refugees still have to financially support their relatives in Bosnia because of the country's terrible economy. This is is just another burden on the lives of many Bosnian immigrants. For instance, for the past few years, Denisa Mutapčić has brought her mother to live with her and her children for a few months every year, instead of sending money to her mother in Bosnia. This way, she said, "We can all spend more time with each other for a few months every year. When she is with us, I can see her every day and night, talk to her and not miss her that much. My kids also can be around their grandmother and get to know her better."[33] Denisa has three children and as she further explains, she cannot afford to buy five tickets for her children and her husband to go to visit Bosnia every year. But this way, she buys only one ticket for her mother and she can stay a few months with them.

Figure 1.8. Denisa Mutapčić with her mother Keti Kuduzović and her daughter Vanesa at Niagara Falls during her mother's visit to America in 2016.

33. Denisa Mutapčić, personal interview with author, November 11, 2014.

"We both feel much better, since my mother started coming every year for a few months to visit us. She likes it here but can't stay for long since she misses my brother and his family who still live in Bosnia. Also, since my sister's tragic death, my mother is taking care of her son, my nephew."[34]

Regardless of how Bosnian refugees choose to deal with their older parents, siblings, relatives who still live in Bosnia, they are heavily on their minds and in their hearts. Even after twenty years since the war ended in Bosnia, they are still loyal to their extended families. They love them and miss them and most of them are doing everything in their power to keep these relations alive. Unfortunately, Bosnia and Herzegovina still ranges among the ten poorest countries in Europe and even after twenty years, these refugees who are now Rochester residents still financially support and help their families in Bosnia and Herzegovina.

List of Top Ten Poorest European Countries 2016		
Country	Capital	GDP (Per Capita) (USD)
Moldova	Chişinău	$2,560
Ukraine	Kiev	$3,560
Kosovo	Priština	$3,990
Albania	Tirana	$4,450
Bosnia and Herzegovina	Sarajevo	$4,760
Macedonia	Skopje	$5,150
Serbia	Belgrade	$5,820
Montenegro	Podgorica	$7,320
Bulgaria	Sofia	$7,620
Romania	Bucharest	$9,520

Table 1.1. Bosnia and Herzegovina among the 10 poorest countries in Europe. Source:http://gazettereview.com/2016/02/top-ten-poorest-countries-europe/

---

34. Ibid.

Even though Bosnia and Herzegovina, even prior to the war, was a poor country, the majority of Bosnian refugees residing in Rochester, New York tend to idealize the life they had in Bosnia. Usually, the life in Bosnia prior to the war was described as good and happy, surrounded by friends and family and without economic or social hardship. Another issue that has emerged among the first-generation Bosnian refugees is the rising divorce rates. Many Bosnian women initiate divorce, using the support and tools provided by their adopted homeland. This new phenomenon has surfaced in the Rochester Bosnian community within the last decade, a practice that is still on the rise. Much of this increase can be attributed to the recognition of the maltreatment women in Bosnia had to endure. Early years for Bosnian Refugees in America were met with nights spent in prison for domestic abuse, as husbands physically abused their wives, a practice they had never been held accountable for in Bosnia. Moving to America provided these women a means of escape. A Bosnian woman, who does not want to disclose her full identity, described her divorce process in the following manner:

> Even in Bosnia, I wanted to get a divorce because my husband was abusive, but I did not want to bring shame to my family, especially to my parents. I promised to myself, that I would stay married, no matter the difficulties and do my best to maintain the marriage, only to keep my parents and kids happy. However, my marriage was unbearable. When my husband drank too much alcohol, he verbally and physically abused me on a daily basis, because he was so insanely jealous. He would then strike me for no reason. When we moved to United States, I hoped he would change, yet he continued drinking alcohol heavily. He tried to hit me on several occasions, but my sons did not allow him.
>
> They said they would call the police if he tried again, and told him that we were no longer in Bosnia where as a husband could do as he pleased. The laws in the United States are much different, and women have rights.

He stopped abusing me physically, but the verbal abuse never stopped. After a few years of living in Rochester, our marriage was over. Therefore, I initiated divorce and we have legally divorced. My kids were old enough, 22 and 20 years old, and they understood. They told me they would prefer if I got married again and began a new happy life, because they would go to college and eventually form their own families.

Now I am married to a great man who appreciates me. He is not a Bosnian man. He is an American, a caring man who loves and respects me. I know some Bosnians disagree with my choice and that they talk behind my back, but I am fine with that. I did what I thought was best for me. If that is selfish of me, so be it. I want to be happy and have someone next to me who loves and appreciates me. One of my brothers cut all contact with me because I married an American man, but some other siblings are talking to me. My parents died few years ago, I miss them very much, but I do not know if they would approve my second marriage.[35]

Meanwhile, some Bosnian men are leaving their Bosnian wives and community and getting involved in relationships outside the Bosnian culture, usually without getting married. One of them, who recently left his wife and who does not want to disclose his identity, told me: "I still love my wife and my family, but I simply can't live without my American girlfriend. I am deeply in love with her. When I am with her, I am a new, free man. She is all I ever wanted in my life. She understands me and does not judge me, but respects me. She is my partner in life and my soul mate. I want to start a new life without the Bosnian community and all the negativities that come with it."[36]

Even though the institution of marriage is deeply embedded in the Bosnian culture, the younger generation chooses to put off marriage, mostly in pursuit of higher education. Some of them decided to embrace their host country's practice of living with their chosen partners without getting married, despite their parents' strong objection.

---

35 .R.O, personal interview with author, August 2014.
36. Anonymous, personal interview with author, September, 2014.

Another crisis becoming prevalent among Bosnian males is extensive alcohol consumption and drug abuse, which has already caused a few cases of alcohol poisoning, deaths from overdosing, and cases of driving while intoxicated.[37] Although it was not a tradition for Muslim women in Bosnia and Herzegovina to drink alcohol, many of them started consuming alcohol when they arrived in Rochester. According to one of the Bosnian women who agreed to interview, specifically wanting to talk about alcohol abuse, women drinking alcohol started as a special exception during birthday or New Year celebration parties.

Halima Stenaklić is a Bosnian woman who was in one of the first refugee waves and came to Rochester, New York in 1997 with her husband and eleven-month-old baby. She recalls the time when Bosnian men and women would gather at her house and drink alcohol excessively. On the weekends, a group of Bosnian men and women, would come to her house and stay until the next day. She remembers this Bosnian traditional evening parties or gatherings called *Sijela* where men and women would get together each weekend at a different house. The host would prepare great deal of food and buy beer and other alcoholic beverages.

Figure 1.9 Halima Stenaklic with her husband Esad, daughter Selam and Imam Enes Tralješić during her daughter's wedding. May 19th, 2013.

---

37. Author's personal observations and funeral participation.

They would eat and drink the whole night and smoke cigarettes. Usually men would smoke so many cigarettes in the room that people eventually would not be able to see each other. Usually, they would gather on Friday and Saturday night because they would have a Sunday to sleep longer for the following Monday. Halima said; "I did that for many years, but thank God, I am not doing it anymore. No alcohol is allowed in my house any longer. My husband doesn't drink alcohol anymore and our life is better than ever."[38]

Senada Pehlivanović had the same experience and remembered long and sleepless nights, gathering with Bosnians and with a whole variety of food, beers, and cigarettes. She recalls the time when she cooked and prepared food for seventy Bosnian refugees. She wanted to include every single Bosnian refugee residing in Rochester to come and gather at her home. She clearly remembers her daughter's first birthday where she had seventy Bosnian refugees at her home, all from different parts of Bosnia, most of them having never met before coming to Rochester. She said, "Nobody was too religious, we all consumed alcohol and now after almost 20 years of living in Rochester, it is hard for me to recognize some people from our earlier gatherings, especially women. They changed, I guess, for the better. Now they go to the mosque, do not drink alcohol, and observe Ramadan. That is fine, but I have hard time respecting these people who spent many years excessively drinking alcohol in my presence."[39]

Another Bosnian, Faruk Ferizović-Dolić, who came among the first refugees to Rochester, NY, also talked about *Sijela* or gatherings of Bosnian refugees. Some groups would visit each other regularly, every day or night. However, the majority would gather to celebrate children's birthdays or "Bajrams."[40] He also recalls heated debates among Bosnian refugees about whether or not alcohol should be consumed in the first Bosnian club organized by Bosnian refugees in Rochester, NY. In addition, the majority of them voted against alcohol consumption inside the club.[41] Samija Sidran came to Rochester with her family on May 4th, 1994. Her family was the 76th family to arrive in Rochester, NY. Her husband was in a concentration camp, which was how she was able to come to America.

---

38 Halima Stenaklić, personal interview with author, November 11, 2014.
39. Senada Pehlivanović, personal Interview with author, August 14, 2015.
40. Bajrams or Eids are two important religious holidays celebrated by Muslims worldwide that marks the end of Ramadan, the Islamic holy month of fasting (sawm) and "Festival of the Sacrifice." Source: https://en.wikipedia.org/wiki/Eid_al-Adha, retrieved on September 24, 2016.
41. Faruk Ferizović-Dolić, personal Interview with author August 14, 2015.

Her husband's cousin had arrived two months earlier, so she decided to come to Rochester, too. Samija said, "We faced many challenges. When we came to Rochester, we did not know the language, nothing. We were lost, literally. First, we did not even know the other refugees from Bosnia who came before us because we were from different parts of the country. However, we got to know each family; we became like brothers and sisters. We visited each other and we spent a lot of time together. Sadly, that changed. Now it is different."[42]

Besides interviewing Bosnian refugees living in Rochester, NY, a few interviews were conducted with people who were involved in helping Bosnian refugees and who wanted to share their experiences and involvement with Bosnian refugees. One of them is Frank Nadz and here is how Frank describes his way to America and his work with Bosnian refugees.

> My name is Frank Nadz and I came to Rochester in 1964. I am from Čakovo, a small place near Osijek in Croatia. I ran from Tito and his communist party when I was sixteen years old with my friend, who, at the time, was seventeen. On the local TV station I saw that a group of refugees from the former Yugoslavia was coming to Rochester, so I went to the airport to greet and help them. I was very alone here in Rochester and when I saw that refugees were coming I had mixed feelings. I was happy and sad. Happy because I could talk again with somebody in my native language and sad because these people were forced to leave their homes. I understood them completely. I opened up my home, and many single men ended up living in my house. This was a long time ago for now I am seventy-five years old. However, whenever they see me they are extremely happy and thankful. Some of them are still my neighbors. At first, I would find them apartments close to my house so it would be easier on me when I would drive them around to various appointments. It was about fifteen families, and most of them stayed in my neighborhood. They bought houses close to mine, and I am very happy to be able to see them and have them as my neighbors. In addition, there is big building nearby where many elderly Bosnians live. Every week I go there to visit them. They love to see me, and we crack some jokes.[43]

42. Samija Sidran, personal interview with author, August 15, 2015.
43. Frank Nadz, telephone interview with author, December 03, 2014.

CHAPTER TWO

REFUGEES FROM SREBRENICA
AND CONCENTRATION CAMPS

I t is important to note that a large number of Bosnian refugees in Rochester, NY came directly from Serbian-run and Croatian-run concentration camps in Bosnia. Many others came from Srebrenica, a city where
a massive genocide took place under the control of three leaders who committed crimes against humanity in Bosnia and Herzegovina, namely the
former president of Serbia, Slobodan Milosević, the former Bosnian Serb
military leader, Ratko Mladić and a former Bosnian Serb politician, Radovan
Karadzic. In the summer of 1995, in the Bosnian city of Srebrenica, under
their direct orders, their Serb militias massacred over 8,000 Muslim men
and boys.[44]

It is important to mention again, that the Bosnian city of Srebrenica in
1993, during the aggression on Bosnia and Herzegovina between 1992-1995,
was declared a UN Safe Zone and under the direct watch and protection
of the United Nations Protection Force (UNPROFOR). Bosnian Muslims
from neighboring cities and villages gathered inside the safe zone to escape
cold-blooded massacre. Sadly, in July 1995, the United Nations failed to protect Muslims and allowed Bosnian Serbs to invade the "safe zone" to systematically kill men and boys only because they were Muslims. Kofi Annan,
the Secretary-General of the United Nations, described this massacre as a
mass murder that marked the worst crime on European soil since the Second
World War.[45] He also wrote: "'Through error, misjudgment and the inability
to recognize the scope of evil confronting us we failed to do our part to save

44. Christiane Amanpour, *The West cannot stand by in Syria as we did for too long in Bosnia* .source: http://
www.telegraph.co.uk/news/2016/10/04/the-west-cannot-stand-by-in-syria-as-we-did-for-too-long-in-
bosn/, retrieved on October 5, 2016.
45. UN Press Release SG/SM/9993UN, 11/07/2005 "Secretary-General Kofi Annan's message to the cer-
emony marking the tenth anniversary of the Srebrenica massacre in Potocari-Srebrenica."Retrieved on
August 9th, 2010.

Map 1.1 Map of Bosnia and Herzegovina.
Source: United Nations

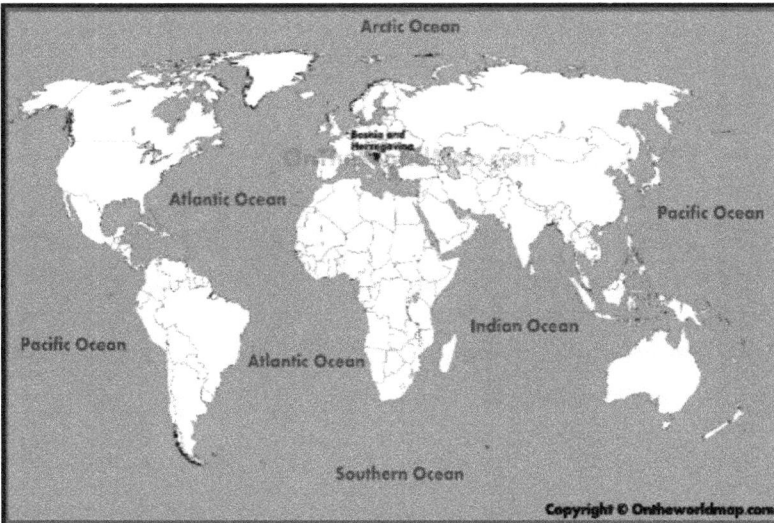

Map 1.2 Bosnia and Herzegovina on
the World map Source: Ontheworldmap.com

the people of Srebrenica from the Serb campaign of mass murder. These failings were in part rooted in a philosophy of neutrality and nonviolence wholly unsuited to the conflict in Bosnia."[46] Additionally, Christiana Amanpour, a CNN correspondent and daughter of an English mother and Iranian father, covered the Bosnian war trying to bring the atrocities happening in Bosnia to the world's attention. She was reporting from Sarajevo when she addressed President Bill Clinton, saying:[47]

> Mr. President, it is a privilege to address you from Sarajevo. You tonight just said that Bosnia was just a humanitarian catastrophe. Surely, sir, you would agree it is so much more than that, a fundamental question of international law and order. You also said that it is clearly in your national interest, the U.S. national interest. So my question is, as leader of the free world, as leader of the only superpower, why has it taken you, the United States, so long to articulate a policy on Bosnia? Why, in the absence of a policy, have you allowed the U.S. and the West to be held hostage to those who do have a policy – the Bosnian Serbs – and do you not think that the constant flip-flops of your Administration on the issue of Bosnia set a very dangerous precedent and would lead people such as Kim Il Sung or other strong people to take you less seriously than you would like to be taken?" "No, but speeches like that may make them take me less seriously than I'd like to be taken," he snapped back. And then, with his jaw stiffening, he added, "There have been no constant flip-flops, madam.[48]

Christiane Amanpour understood right away that the Bosnian conflict was not a civil war but a result of Serbian aggression. She strongly believed that what the "world community should have done is act on its own principles,"[49] as did Margaret Thatcher, a former Prime Minister of Britain, when she said "Stop the Excuses. Help Bosnia Now."[50]

46. Barbara Crossette. "U.N. Details Its Failure to Stop '95 Bosnia Massacre." (New York Time: NOV. 16, 1999).+ Source: http://www.nytimes.com/1999/11/16/world/un-details-its-failure-to-stop-95-bosnia-massacre.html?_r=0. Retrieved on September, 14 2016.Source: https://www.srebrenica.org.uk/.
47. Stephen Kinzer, "Where There's War There's Amanpour." Published: October 9, 1994.source: http://www.nytimes.com/1994/10/09/magazine/where-there-s-war-there-s-amanpour.html?pagewanted=all.
48. Ibid.
49. Ibid.
50. Margaret Thatcher. *Stop the excuses. Help Bosnia now. Source: New York Times, 6 August 1992*.http://www.margaretthatcher.org/document/108299. Retrieved on. December 31, 2016.

Figure 2.1. Christiane Amanpour, 1994: Amanpour questions Bill Clinton at CNN forum in 1994, Christiane Amanpour questioned then-President Bill Clinton's policy 'flip-flops' in Bosnia. Source: CNN

In July of 1995, The Army of Republica Serpska, under the command of General Ratko Mladić, split the Bosnian Muslim Community in the city of Srebrenica along gender lines and perpetrated the historic massacre. Over eight thousand boys and adult men, 8,373 to be exact, were killed in the span of a few days.[51] Luckily, a few managed to escape this atrocity. Among them was a famous Bosnian national soccer player, Vedad Ibisevic, a star striker in the German club Hertha BSC, who was only seven years old when his family fled the atrocity of war in Bosnia. "Twenty-two years ago", he recalls, "over a four-month period, Serb neighbors invaded my mother's village, Pijuke, and called out familiar names on a bullhorn, promising that no one would be hurt. They murdered everyone who emerged."[52]

51. Norman Cigar, *Genocide in Bosnia: The Policy of Ethnic Cleansing*. TX: Texas A and M University Press, 2000).
52. Wright Thompson. "Nothing Can Stay Buried" *ESPN The Magazine 23-1426*. (May 2014). Source: Source: http://www.espn.com/espn/feature/story/_/id/10921287/nothing-stay-buried-bosnia-herzegovina-forward-vedad-ibisevic-returns-homeland.

Figure 2.2. Refugees looking through barbed wire in Srebrenica, Bosnia in 1995 Credit: -/ APsource: http://www.telegraph.co.uk/news/2016/10/04/the-west-cannot-stand-by-in-syria-as-we-did-for-too-long-in-bosn/.

Figure 2.3. Dutch U.N. peacekeepers sit on top of an armored personnel carrier while Muslim refugees from Srebrenica gather in the village of Potocari on July 13, 1995. Source: http://www.theatlantic.com/photo/2015/07/20-years-since-the-srebrenica-massacre/398135/.

Figure 2.4. July 13, 1995: Bosnian Muslim refugees flee Srebrenica Source: Reuters.

The ethnic-cleansing militia tortured and killed as many Muslims as they could find, burning down every house. They split his grandfather's head open and carved a cross into the chest of a local shop owner, a man who kept chocolate in his store for children like Vedad.[53] All this happened under the United Nations' watchful eyes of Dutch peacekeepers. In April 1993, the United Nations declared the besieged enclave of Srebrenica a "safe zone" under United Nations' protection.[54] Indeed, July 1995, the United Nations Protection Force (UNPROFOR), represented on the ground in Srebrenica numbered 500-strong contingent of Dutch peacekeepers. This strong contingent was compromised and did not prevent the town's capture and subsequent massacre.[55] Between 1992 and 1995, over 100,000 Bosnians were killed and half of the country's population was turned into refugees, including Ibisević and his family.[56]

54 .Mike Corder (20 August 2006). "*Srebrenica Genocide Trial to Restart*". The Washington Post. Retrieved: October 26, 2010.
55. Corder, ibid.
56. Ibid.

Figure 2.5. Vedad Ibišević of Bosnia and Herzegovina celebrates scoring his team's first goal during the 2014 FIFA World Cup Brazil on June 15, 2014 in Rio de Janeiro, Brazil.(Photo: Julian Finney/Getty Images) Source:http://www.zimbio.com/photos/Vedad Ibisević.

Bosnia-Herzegovina has endured many attacks from its neighbors, with an increased pressure starting when the Ottoman Empire collapsed and left Bosnian Muslims without protection. Many wars have been launched against Bosnians, forcing Bosnian Muslims to seek refuge in other countries and leave behind everything they have. Bosnian Muslims have been trapped between two nationalistic neighbors: from the east, Serbian Orthodox Christians and from the west and north, Croatian Catholics. However, none of these previous attacks were so brutal and widespread as the latest. In 1992, the Ibisević family found itself in one of the most vicious conflicts in the region's history, one that would claim an estimated 100,000 lives before it ended in 1995.[57]

Prince Zeid Ra'ad Zeid al-Hussein, who served at the United Nations as a high commissioner for human rights for twenty years, recalls his visit to Bosnia and Herzegovina. A United Nations convoy was in transit when the car of a Bosnian Serb paramilitary fighter pulled alongside, and on its hood was the severed head of a Bosnian Muslim child adorned with a United Nations peacekeeper's blue helmet. That episode and the plight of two young girls shot by a sniper in Sarajevo have left him decades later still asking; "How can you comprehend this?"[58]

---

57 Thompson, ibid.
58. Nick Cumming-Bruce U.N. *Rights Chief Says He'll Shine a Light on Countries Big and Small* (June, 2015). Source: http://www.nytimes.com/2015/01/31/world/un-rights-chief-to-shine-light-on-countries-big-and-small.html. Retrieved January 1st, 2015.

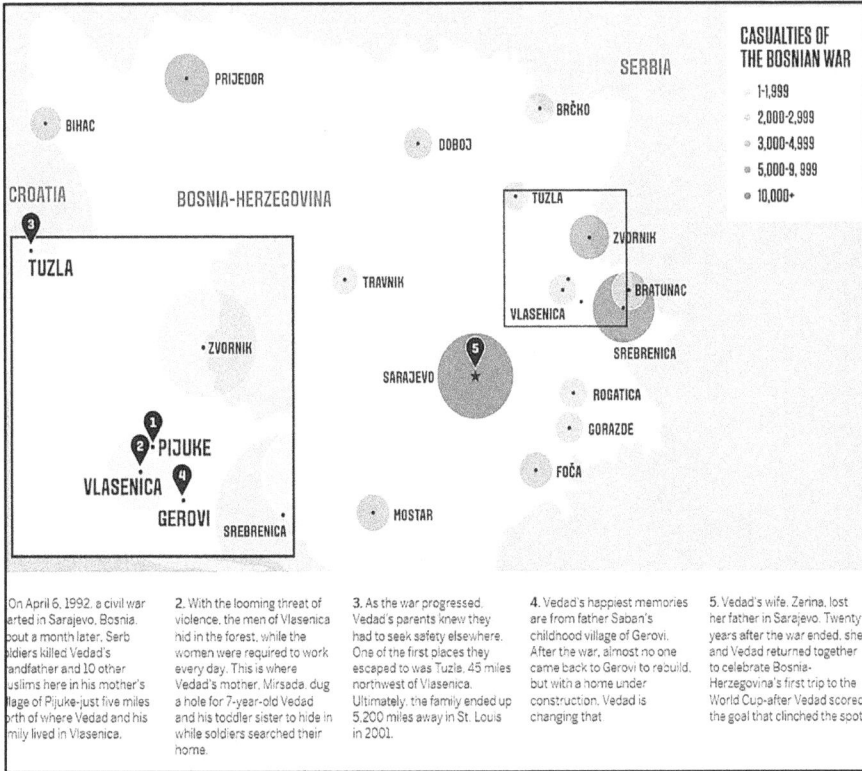

Map 2.1. Casualties of the Bosnian War, Pijuke, village where Vedad Ibišević was born.

Twenty years ago, around 15,000 people, mostly men and boys but also women, children and the elderly fled Srebrenica. The majority of these were killed in minefields or during bombings and ambushes. According to survivors' testimonies, only 3,500 managed to survive. They had to walk through the forest for days without food, eating leaves to survive while caring for their children and elderly. All the while poisonous gas was being dropped on them and they passed many dead bodies. Meho Kapidzić, was one of the survivors. He was born in Glogova, a village near the city of Bratunac, Bosnia and Herzegovina, and he is a Bosnian refugee who escaped this fate. Meho ended up in Rochester and embraced the city as his new home. In a personal interview on January 14th, 2015, he described his escape as follows:

Figure 2.6. International War Crimes Tribunal investigators clear away soil and debris from dozens of Srebrenica victims buried in a mass grave near the village of Pilica, 55 kilometers northeast of Tuzla, on September 18th, 1996. #Station R. Winter / AP
Source:http://www.theatlantic.com/photo/2015/07/20-years-since-the-srebrenica massacre/398135/.

My name is Meho Kapidžić and I was born in Glogova, Bratunac in Bosnia. From my birth until the beginning of the war in Bosnia I lived in my village Glogova. On May 9th, 1992 I left my home with my wife and my newly born daughter, along with my father, my two brothers, my mother, my pregnant sister and my sister in law with her son. From 1992 on, our Muslim villages around Srebrenica were under constant attack by Serb forces. For three days and nights we hid in the woods and on the fourth day we decided to go towards Srebrenica because it was a "Free Zone" or "Safe Haven." On the way to Srebrenica, we crossed one village called Milacevici, but there was nothing there, so the next day we went to village called Sušnjari.

In that village we found some food. We all stayed and lived in just one room. One of my brothers soon left afterwards to join the fighting. We stayed there for a month; afterwards we managed to reach Srebrenica where we lived in a apartment until the end of 1992.

We left Srebrenica because we didn't have anything to eat and decided to go towards another city, called Konjović Polje. My brother with his wife and kid went to live with her parents and again my wife, daughter, father, mother and pregnant sister and I lived in my father's friend's house with whom he had worked in Germany. We stayed there for about four months and again from Konjović Polje we went back to a village close to our home. My father stayed with the women and kids and as boys, while the three brothers went to the village and tried with our army to get it back from Serbs.

Finally my village was free, but not for long. Serbain nationalists regained control over my village again. We went back again to Srebrenica thinking that we would be safe there. That was around the time when General Philippe Morillon of France, Commander of the United Nations Protection Force (UNPROFOR), visited Srebrenica and told us that the city is under United Nations' protection and that he would protect us. He also insisted that women and children leave Srebrenica because the life was impossible there, lacking running water, food, medication etc. Only women left Srebrenica, most men and boys stayed in Srebrenica until July 1995. My mother didn't want to leave us, but my wife with our daughter and my sister and sister in law went to Tuzla and we communicated via letters that we exchanged through the Red Cross.

I just wanted to say that my daughter Meliha had her first birthday in the woods, under a large tree. That was very difficult and hardbreaking for all of us, and affected my father the most. He told me that he worked very hard in Germany and saved money for his family so that they would have a nice life, and yet, here he was with his family and his first granddaughter, on her fist birthday, in the woods, having nothing and powerless to protect them.

In Srebrenica we stayed until July 1995 and I called it Black July. Life was very hard in Srebrenica. We didn't have enough food and we lived in a garage; my mother, father and us three sons. There was no food in Srebrenica. The Serbs' forces were controlling all access roads and they didn't allow anyone in or out Srebrenica. They didn't allow international humanitarian aid either, including food and medicine to reach Srebrenica. Somehow, through the woods, we managed to get to neighboring city Žepa to search for food, sometimes getting lucky and bringing home some food, but most of the time, we risked our lives for nothing.

Many people died searching for food. By then the humanitarian situation of the Muslim civilians and military personnel in the enclave was catastrophic. Many people died from starvation. Then came July 11, 1995, a day I will never forget. On that day a heavy attack came from the Serbian forces; in fact, the attack had started before. Our army was pushed back, and we didn't have a chance against the Serbs, since they outnumbered us and we were already running out of supplies. The women and children from surrounding villages and cities, who came to Srebrenica seeking UNPROFOR protection crowded the streets. It was a chaotic situation. In my opinion, at that point, UNPROFOR was powerless.

They asked NATO for help, an airstrike to protect the city, but that never happened. The Serbs took charge and control over the city. When we realized that we were not getting help and protection from UNPROFOR forces, men went west, towards the woods while women and kids went east, heading towards Potočcari, another United Nations compound. For many people that was the last time they saw their relatives. Later, I heard from my relatives who went to Potocari, they arrived on the same night, on July 11th 1995, mostly women and kids, around 25,000 at Potocari hoping to get protection within the UN compound there. They wanted to go inside the UN compound, but the Dutch soldiers wouold not allow them.

They claimed that the compound was already full; the Dutch forces were even expelling other refugees who were already inside the compound, having Serbs to do to them whatever they wanted. Among them were women, kids, and unarmed men. Serbs had open hands to do whatever they wanted. They raped girls and young women, killed men and kids, even babies when they cried, all this in front of Dutch soldiers, who did nothing. Meanwhile, my brother and I went to the woods with other men and we were under constant attack from Serbian forces who were waiting for us everywhere.

Figure 2.7. Meho Kapidzić at the Potočari Memorial Complex near Srebrenica.

Figure 2.8. Aiša Purak addressing the Bosnians during the Commemorated Victims of Srebrenica in the Bosnian Mosque in Rochester- July 11th, 2015.

Figure 2.9. Bosnians Commemorated Victims of Srebrenica in the Bosnian Mosque in Rochester- July 11th, 2015.

Figure 2.10. Bosnians Commemorated Victims of Srebrenica in the Bosnian Mosque in Rochester- July [11], 2015.

After a few days we met with our father in Lipa, who had left Srebrenica a few days earlier in order to search for my youngest brother. He didn't feel well, and he told us that he couldn't make it. We talked for over two hours and he told us to go together, but advised us not to walk too close to each other, in the case of mines or snipers, at least one could survive. He couldn't find our youngest brother since we hadn't heard from him in over ten days, so he thought that he was already killed. My father told us that he was old and wouldn't be killed, so he would go to the UNPROFOR "safe zone" where he would be safe. After that, my father went towards Potočari, UNPROFOR compound and my brother and I went towards Tuzla using the so-called "Bloody Road." That was the last time we saw him. On the way to Tuzla, my brother went missing. It took eighteen years to find and indentify both of my brothers and properly bury them. Now at least we know where they are and we can go and visit their graves.[59]

59. Meho Kapidzić, telephone interview with author, January 15, 2015.

One of the Srebrenica's survivors, Hasiba Gobeljic, who, with her family, lives in Rochester, NY, talked about her devastating experience in Srebrenica. She remembers very well when General Ratko Mladic with his Army of Republica Srpska entered city of Srebrenica and started dividing men and boys from their mothers, sisters and wives. She recalls clearly the moment when "Ratko Mladic came to us, women and children and asked us, "Where is your president now? Where is your Alija Izetbegoivc? He sold you, he does not care about you? Only I can help you now."[60]

On Monday, April 7th, 2014, in the Hague, Netherlands, a civil case was started because of the Bosnian mothers and widows of men and boys murdered in Srebrenica 1995. They sued the Dutch government for failing to protect their husbands and sons serving as United Nations peacekeepers. "I wish the Netherlands would finally take responsibility for these events," said Munira Subasic, the head of Mothers of Srebrenica, which represents some 6,000 widows and victims' relatives. "This is also an opportunity for the Dutch people to recognize the responsibility of their politicians and soldiers in the genocide of Srebrenica," added Subasić. "This is also an opportunity for the [Dutch] ministry of defense to reclaim their military honor."[61] However, the Dutch government claimed it had no control over the troops, instead they were part of a UN peacekeeping mission in Srebrenica. Ultimately, litigant mothers and widows of men and boys murdered in Srebrenica 1995 under Dutch protection lost the civil case.[62]

It is important to mention that in 2013, a year prior to this case, mothers of Srebrenica launched a case against the UN at the European Court for Human Rights, but this attempt also failed due to immunity for peacekeeping forces.[63]

---

60. Hasiba Gobeljic, conversation with the author during Ramadan 2016 at the Bosnia Cultural Center.
61. Deutsche Welle, "Srebrenica relatives sue Dutch government."(Date 07.04.2014) Source: http://www.dw.de/srebrenica-relatives-sue-dutch-government/a-17549521, retrieved September 21,2015.
62. Ibid.
63. Ibid.

RAPE AS AN ACT OF GENOCIDE IN BOSNIA AND HERZEGOVINA FROM 1992-1995

T he phrase "to the victor go the spoils" writes Kelly Down Askin in her book *War Crimes Against Women: Prosecution in International War Crimes Tribunals.*[64] Furthermore, Angela Robinson, a London based journalist specializing in human rights, issues a similar statement. "If human rights are to be universally respected and protected, they must apply to the lives of over half the human race women."[65] Additionally, Susan Brownmiller *in* her book, *Against Our Will: Men, Women and Rape*, points out that the victim is not guilty of rape but rather the perpetrator.[66] Hillary Clinton, in her speech given as First Lady of the United States on September 5th 1995, at the *United Nations* Fourth World Conference on Women in Beijing said: "Human rights are women's rights, and women's rights are human rights."[67] However, reality for women is much different, especially during wartime.

According to Brownmiller, rape in wartime has been the common experience of women from all over the world since the first wars broke out. It has occurred in all civilizations, but different civilizations had different approaches and sanctions concerning this crime. Genocide, as well as the element of rape in genocide, does not just emerge spontaneously, but is a manifestation of specific government policies with the intention of achieving certain political goals. The genocide in Bosnia and Herzegovina is no exception to this rule. Genocide is in fact a planned crime at the state level and would not be possible without a strong, planned military power behind it.[68]

---

64. Kelly Dawon Askin, *War Crimes Against Women: Prosecution in International War Crimes Tribunals* (Martinus: Nijhoff Publishers.1997), pg. 10.
65. Robinson, Angela, *Weapon of War*, New Internationalist magazine. Source: http://www.org/features/1993/06/05/rape/.
66. Susan Brownmiller, Against Our Will (New York: Simon and Schuster, 1975).
67 .Gertrude Fester, *Agenda: Empowering Women for Gender Equity No. 20, Politics, Power and Democracy* (Abingdon: Taylor & Francis, Ltd. 1994), pg. 76-79.
68. Brownmiller, ibid.

In the wars against Bosnia and Herzegovina and its society, the state of Serbia, Montenegro and Croatia, and their militaristic and paramilitary structures, carried out the genocide against Bosniaks throughout history and used rape as a tool to achieve their goal.[69]

Brownmiller argues that the history of rape as an act of genocide is as old as the history of warfare. The history of genocide as viewed from a world - historical context, reveals the astounding fact that the history of man, among other things, is based primarily on wars, genocide, persecution, hunger, and other forms of suffering. This is simply a cemetery of missing nations and cultures. Indeed, human history has a brighter side, the side of peace, work, prosperity. This is, however, certainly unfinished and never lasting. Another important fact reveals to us a historical description of wars and genocide. It is a fact that in all wars and genocidal processes, the state and its military power play a key part. Almost until the end of the 20th century, rape in war had rarely been documented and therefore remained invisible and unpunished.[70] The rape of women has been utilized as a terror tactic in wars since the beginning of armed conflict and, according to Robinson, there are three main types. First, rape is routine and an expected reward to the victors. Second, rape occurs due to a lack of military discipline. Finally, rape occurs as a military technique to demoralize the opposition. Through these horrific actions, women experience the loss of home and the loss of land, which is synonymous with the loss of identity.[71]

It is also important to point to the undeniable fact that in an attempt to implement the project of Greater Serbia or Greater Croatia at the expense of Bosnian territory, neighboring countries Serbia and Croatia also used the act of rape in their process of eliminating Bosniaks and Bosnian society.[72] As a part of "ethnic cleansing" by Serbs in their genocidal war with Bosnia, in 1992 they began the massive rape of women in Bosnia.

69. Amnesty International, "Bosnia-Herzegovina: Rape and Sexual Abuse by Armed Forces."1993. Source:https://www.amnesty.org/download/Documents/188000/eur630011993en.pd. Retrieved,October 25,2015.
70. Brownmiller, ibid.
71. Angela,Robinson, *Religious Tolerance: Rape of women during wartime* (Ontario: Consultants on Religious Tolerance ,2002),pg. 32.
72. Beverly Allen. Rape Warfare: *The Hidden Genocide in Bosnia-Herzegovina and Croatia,* (Minneapolis: University Of Minnesota Press,1996).

Amnesty International has confirmed that 20,000 Muslim girls and women have been raped in Bosnia since the fighting began in April 1992.[73] Teenage girls have been a particular target in Bosnia and Herzegovina and Croatia, according to The State of the World's Children 1996 report. The report also says that impregnated girls were forced to bear "the enemy's" child and were held captive until termination of pregnancy was too late.[74]

Extreme violence against Bosnian Muslim women was perpetrated to shame and intimidate Muslim families – especially men. Rape was used to humiliate and degrade Muslim women. They were held as slaves, forced to cook and clean and used as sex slaves. Serbian nationalists viewed Muslim women as their property and they were sold and given as gifts amongst each other.[75] Many agencies reported that Serbs raped Muslim women and girls in front of their families, making them watch.[76] According to Beverly Allan, who wrote a book titled *Rape Warfare: The Hidden Genocide in Bosnia-Herzegovina and Croatia,* rape in Bosnia was ordered and encouraged from the top Serbian Military leadership to perpetuate genocide forcing Muslim women to bear Serb children "little Serbs" or "a military policy of rape for the purpose of genocide. He concludes that hidden genocide in Bosnia and Croatia becomes thus ugly and barbarian aspect of Serbian War on Bosnians."[77] He concludes that "It is extremely difficult to write about these things. Every phrase risks misinterpretation, every analytic moment risks being incomplete."[78]

Because of the Bosnian Muslims' faith, argue Rittner and Roth, the rape is used to humiliate male family members by demonstrating their apparent inability to protect their women. In Bosnia and Herzegovina, this is especially vicious because of the honor shame complex, characterized by the chastity of females, is fundamental to both individual families and the community as a whole.

---

73. International Criminal Court: Amnesty International, 5 May 2010. Web. 11 Dec. 2010. Retrieved from http://www.amnesty.org/en/ /info/IOR53/009/2010/en.
74. Kathleen Barry, *The Prostitution of Sexuality* (New York and London: New York University Press. 1995),pg. 124.
75. Carol Rittner & John K. Roth, Rape: *Weapon of War and Genocide* (Minnesota: Paragon House. 2012),pg, 47.
76. Ibid., pg, 47.
77. Allen, Ibid.
78. Ibid, pg. xviii.

The rape of women during armed conflicts is a war tactic and a threat to international security because of its psychological nature and the physical abuse of wom- en destroys the entire community.[79] Between 1992 and 1995, a series of armed conflicts erupted after the Yugoslav federation fell apart and its repub- lics began declaring independence. The Bosnian War was the bloodiest. According to the UN, between 20,000 and 50,000 Bosnian wom- en were raped by Serbs—many in special rape camps and took more than 100,000 lives.[80] The event of a rape as an act of genocide against Bosniaks and Bosnian-Herzegovinian society points to the vital need of an all-inclusive explanation for each aspect.

First, it is necessary to comprehensively elucidate the socio-political causes of the genocide, and to point to the multitude of perpetrators of geno-cidal acts, which certainly includes the State as a subject of genocide.[81] Even though rape has been a part of war as long as war has been a part of human existence, and though rape has long been acknowledged as an atrocity, rape did not become a war crime until the late 1990s. Until the war in Bosnia and Herzegovina, the international community failed to effectively identify and recognize the problem of rape of women as one of the acts of genocide that is used during war as a method of achieving its war goals and punishing the men of their counterparts.

Women of Bosnia also made determined efforts to make "mass rape" a crime against humanity punishable by The War Crimes Tribunal. Sadly, that was not the case before the war in Bosnia. Thanks to Bosnian rape victims who bravely and openly spoke out about their horrifying experiences, the International War Crimes Tribunal now recognizes "mass rape" as a punish-able crime against humanity, while until 1992 rape during the war was seen as a side effect of the war and was not a punishable crime against humanity.[82]

---

79. Carol and Roth, Ibid.,pg. 47.
80. Alexandra Stiglmayer. Mass Rape: *the war against women in Bosnia-Herzegovina* (Lincoln: U of Nebraska Press, 1994).
81. Brownmiller, ibid.
82. Claudia Card, "The Paradox of Genocidal Rape Aimed at Enforced Pregnancy" The
The Southern Journal of Philosophy (2008) Vol. XLVI. Source: http://onlinelibrary.wiley.c
doi/10.1111/j.2041-6962.2008.tb00162.x/epdf. Retrieved on November 17, 2016.

Consequently, on December 18th, 1992, the United Nation Security Council declared the "massive, organized and systematic detention and rape of women, in particular Muslim women, in Bosnia and Herzegovina" an international crime that must be addressed.[83] Unfortunately, despite this historical legislation by the UN Security Council, only twelve cases out of an estimated 50,000 have been prosecuted in The Hague in 2010.[84]

---

83. Background Information on Sexual Violence used as a Tool of War. http://www.un.org/en/prevent-genocide/rwanda/about/bgsexualviolence.shtml retrieved on November 17, 2016.
84. Ibid.

CONCENTRATION CAMPS

Even though many Bosnian refugees came to Rochester, NY directly from concentration camps and many agreed to be interviewed, none of them talked about or mentioned being raped or witnessing rape to me. They did, however, talk about other daily abuses. A few Bosnian men came from the Manjača concentration camp that was located on mount Manjača, near the city of Banja Luka. During 1992 Serbs used this concentration camp to imprison Muslim civilians, mostly men between 18 and 60 years old. However, according to survivors there were women held in this camp as well who were repeatedly raped.

Eventually, this camp was shut down in 1993, under international pressure, but was reopened again in October 1995. One of the Bosnian refugees living in Rochester, as a young boy was kept in this concentration camp. He was severely beaten daily, according to another *Manjača* survivor, who does not want to disclose his identity and who himself suffered unbearable headaches because he was repeatedly hit in the head by Serb soldiers. "If I did not take care of him when he arrived in Rochester, he would definitely have ended up in Rochester psychiatric hospital. But I understood him; I knew what he went through. I embraced him like my own family."[85] Sadly, the young boy, who is now man in his late thirties, never recovered from the concentration camp and most of the time needs professional help.

Muharem Kapić is also among the many Bosnian refugees who came to Rochester from the concentration camps. He came from concentration camps run by the Bosnian Croatian Army or the Croatian Defense Council (HVO – Hrvatsko vijeće odbrane).

---

85. Anonymous, personal interview with author, September 2014.

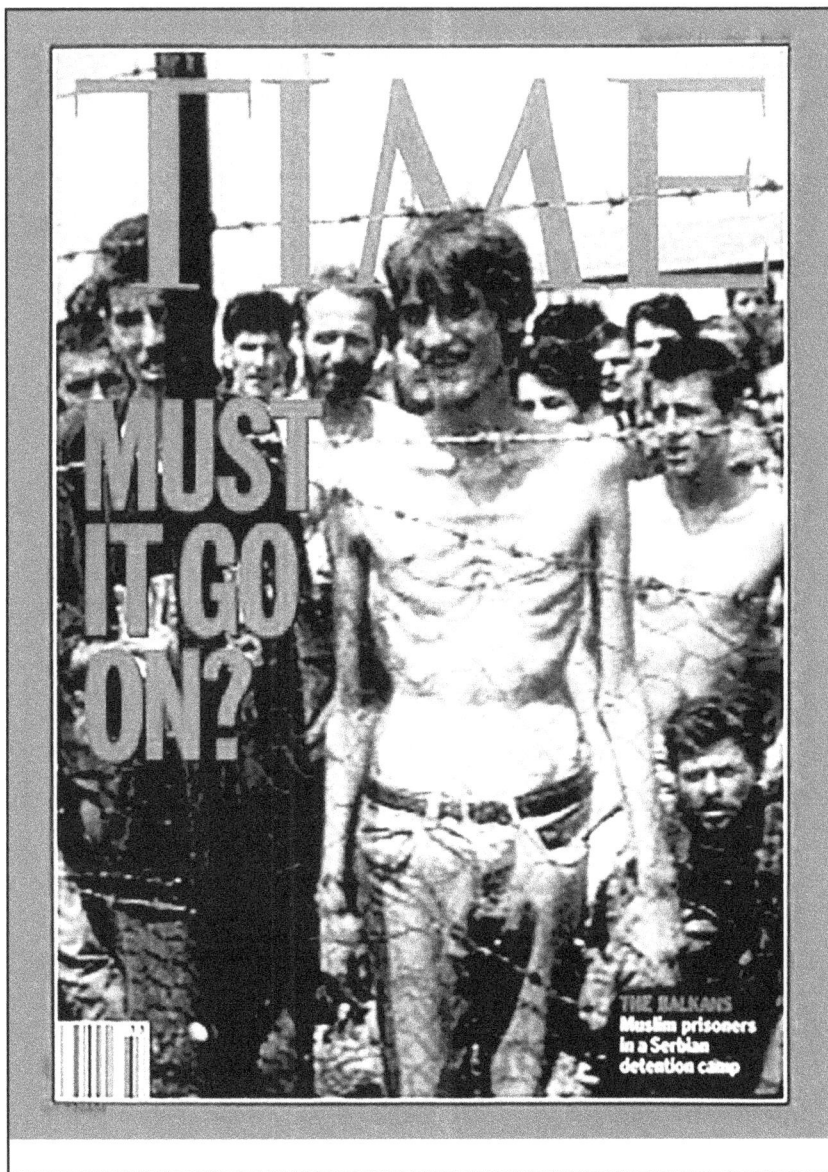

Figure 2.11. Muslim, Fikret Alič, at the Serb-run Trnopolje camp in August 1992Photo: ITN[1]
Source:https://genocideinbosnia.wordpress.com/tag/bosnian-muslims/page/3/.

1 ITN and two of its reporters have won £375,000 in High Court libel damages from a Marxist magazine which claimed they had faked pictures of Bosnian Serb war crimes.
Reporters Penny Marshall and Ian Williams were each awarded £150,000 over the Living Marxism story which called into question ITN's coverage of the Bosnian war.

He was arrested near city of Maglaj in August 1991 because the Bosnian Army was fighting together with the Croatian Army against Serbian force near the city of Maglaj for about seven days. After that, the Croatian Army started fighting together with the Serbian Army against the Bosnian Army, as the Croatian Army had betrayed the Bosnian Army where he was staying. They kept them in a school for seven days, then they transferred all these Bosnians to a concentration camp in Mostar, in a Croat-controlled territory, called Heliodrom.[86] He was there for seven months. Muharem recalls one day in particular:

> One day a group of men came to the camp and I heard them talking in a foreign language and asked if someone wants to go to a different country. Almost all of the people said that we wanted to go back to Bosnia, to our families. They told us that we can't go back to our homes because we killed Croatian and Serb civilians and we are war captives. We can only go to a third country. I asked where can we go and they told me to America and I said I would go. I signed the paper. My neighbors told me not to do that, that we would go back to Bosnia, to our family. However, I signed the paper only to save my life. I wanted to leave that concentration camp because we didn't see food for six days. Also, everyday, they took us to the war zone and we had to work there, make bunkers, dig tunnels. It was miserable to work these hard jobs without seeing food for many days. Whoever refused to go would be killed, plain and simple. That was my chance to leave this camp. Every single minute our lives were in danger.
>
> The concentration camp guards would get drunk, especially during weekends, and they would come inside our camps, and would hit people breaking, their ribs, hands, legs; whomever they saw, they would simply hit the person with their rifles. I couldn't bear the pain and I simply said I wanted to go from here. Many others signed immediately, too. We left Heliodrom camp and they took us to Dretelj camp.[87]

86. The Heliodrom camp (Croatian: Logor Heliodrom) or Heliodrom prison was a detention camp that operated between September 1992 and April 1994. It was run by the Military Police of the Croatian Republic of Herzeg-Bosnia to detain Bosniaks and other non-Croats and was located at a former military facility of the JNA in Rodoč, south of the town of Mostar. Source: https://en.wikipedia.org/wiki/Heliodrom_camp,
retrieved on December 23, 2016.
87. The Dretelj camp or Dretelj prison was a prison camp run by the Croatian Defence Forces (HOS) and later by the Croatian Defence Council (HVO) during the Bosnian War.

The concentration camp was by run by the Croatian Defense Force. They told us from here we will go to the third country. When we arrived there they put us inside garages from the former Yugoslav Army where they kept tanks and we did not see if it was day or night. We met with other Bosnian prisoners who were there before us and they told us that for about six months, they did not have enough water or food. Many prisoners died from starvation. They had not recalled the last time they had bathed.

For nearly half a year, they hadn't even washed their faces. Never will I forget that place. My group did not stay there for long. One day, the garage door opened and we saw daylight. There were a few people standing in front of the door. One woman was talking in a foreign language and others were listening to her. After that, another woman told us that we need to listen carefully for our name, and come outside if our name is called. Next to them, I saw trucks parked with UNICAF name on it, it was about 20 trucks and we were told to go inside these trucks after we heard our name called. After some time, all of the trucks were filled with prisoners. They took us toward Ploce, a city in Croatia. However, when we came close to the border with Croatia, they did not let us in for six hours. We heard people walking around trucks and chanting "We need to throw them all into Neretva river." After some time, we started talking to the guards and they told us that they would take us first to another city, Osjek and we would stay there for some time to recover, and then we would go to a third country.[88]

Muharem stayed in Split for an hour and then he was transported to city of Osijek. On December 25th, 1993 he arrived in Osijek, Croatia around 8 at night. He remembers the time and date of his arrival very well because there was so much gunfire. The Croats were Croats celebrating Christmas. In his group were about 600 Bosnians who arrived with him. In Osjek there were already 7000 refugees, mostly Bosnians, but also Croats who had to leave their homes because of Serbian occupation. It was much better for Muharem in Osjek.

Source: https://en.wikipedia.org/wiki/Dretelj_camp, retrieved on December 23, 2016.
88. Muharem Kapić, personal interview with author December 02, 2014.

He was given a small home, brand new with a good shower and a lot of food and clothing. "It was very good I could eat as much as I wanted," Muharem said. His two sons were in Split, Croatia and he managed to bring them to Osjek as well. Meanwhile, his wife and daughter were still in Bosnia; they had not heard from him since his capture.

The following year, on March 20th, 1994, he left Osjek and took a flight to United States with his two sons. Eventually he landed in Rochester, NY. With him were his two sons and two other Bosnians who had been in concentration camps with him, Semso and Avdo Kezo who were from Mostar. While in the Heliodrom concentration camp, they were able to see their own house in Mostar from the camp where they were kept by their neighbors, the Croats. Their sponsor was Turkish Imam Mehmed Baktas who had already sponsored a few Bosnian families earlier. During their first meeting at the airport, Vardar Sulejman was their translator. He was originally from Macedonia and he had already lived in Rochester for 30 years.

They were taken to a house of a Turkish man named Hamza, where ate before being taken to another house located on Clinton Avenue. When they arrived inside the house they were told not to open the curtains on the windows in the morning. Muharmen, the oldest son, understood a little bit of English; when asked why, they just said not to open the curtains in the morning. They were very tired from the flight and slept, but in the morning, Muharem went to the window and saw that a bullet had been fired on this house and the window was damaged. He could not believe what was happening to him, his sons, and Semso and Avdo in America, on their first day in Rochester. NY. They were alone in the empty house and somebody had shot at the house where they were staying. They slept in the living room, all of them. The next morning, the Turkish imam Mehmed delivered food, blankets, pillows, mattresses, and water.

They had two rooms and a kitchen, and now had mattresses, pillows, and blankets. It was good. They were also taken to finish the paper work and soon they started getting food stamps and health coverage. After that, it was even better. They stayed there for about six months. Imam Mehmed helped them send papers to his wife and daughter, who arrived six months after. After his wife and daughter arrived, they moved to a different place.

However, his wife was not happy here in Rochester. Patricia (Patty) Reed, an American woman, was helping both the Kapić family and other Bosnian refugees as well. According to Dr. Emir Ramić,[89]

Chairman of the Institute for Research of Genocide Canada, from an interview he gave to the prominent Bosnian web magazine Bosnjaci Net, the massive and individual murders of Bosniaks in the Republic of Bosnia and Herzegovina between 1992 - 1995 occurred mostly in the concentration camps, though also in other detention facilities, located in: sports centers, schools, hospitals, recreational and catering facilities, factory floors, military barracks, movie theaters, police stations, hotels, correctional centers - state prisons, hangars, concrete bunkers, tunnels, warehouses, distribution centers, mines, ancient caves, etc. In his interview he also provided a summary of casualties and injuries from the 10th genocide against Bosniaks:

Figure 2.13. Muharem Kapić with his wife Rafija and his two sons.
From the Left: Hilmo, Rafija, Muharem and Omer on Greater Rochester International Airport. Muharem with his wife Rafija were among first Bosnians from Rochester community to traveling to Meka to perform Hajj, or pilgrimage on September 2015.

89 Dr. Emir Ramić is a Chairman of the Institute for Research of Genocide Canada He becomes political and educational voice for the Bosnian Americans and Canadians in assisting the Bosnian Americans and Canadians in learning the cultural, economic, legal, political, and social systems of the United States and Canada. He helps and assists United States and Canada foreign policy in Balkans so that Bosnia & Herzegovina and its people are never again the target of aggression and genocide. Source: http://nedira-jtebosnu.net/?view=naucna_istrazivanja&id=184.

Figure 2.13. Panel discussion on active role of Bosnian women and their participation in Bosnian community in America and Canada. Participants: from the left: Aiša Purak, Imam Tajib ef. Pašanbegović, Dr. Emir Ramić and Mr. Azra Durić in Guelph, City in Ontario, Canada on September 13th, 2015.

- Number of killed Bosniaks exceeds 200,000 of which over 22,000 were children;
- Number of wounded: 240,000, of which 52,000 were children;
- Number of handicapped: 100,600, of which over 4,000 were children;
- Number displaced: 1,225,000, in over a hundred countries around the world;
- Number displaced within Bosnia and Herzegovina: 850,000;
- Number of raped women: 40,000;
- Number of missing persons: 53,600, of which 28,420 were from Srebrenica and Žepa;
- Number of villages that were completely destroyed: 475.

CHAPTER THREE

HISTORY OF BOSNIA AND HERZEGOVINA

For a better understanding of Bosnian Americans, their cultural and religious background, this work will give a detailed overview of their history, focusing on the atrocities from 1992 to 1995, which had directly impacted their past, present and future. Bosnia and Herzegovina, a Southeastern European country, is located on the western coast of the Balkan Peninsula bordering Serbia and Montenegro to the East, Croatia to the North and West, with a narrow exit to the Adriatic Sea. From the last census from 2013 there were 3,531,159 people living in Bosnia and Herzegovina.[90] The Bosnian population is both ethnically and religiously divided with 50.11% Bosniaks-Muslim, 15.43% Croats-Roman Catholic, and 30.78% Serbs-Orthodox, with 0.77% of the population choosing to not express their ethnic background or religious beliefs. All three groups speak the same language, although they are called by different names: Bosnian, Croatian, and Serbian, respective to their ethnic division.[91]

Bosnians are a unique component of the American melting pot because of their European roots and the Islamic faith. Illyrians were the earliest inhabitants of Bosnia and Herzegovina of whom historical records exist. Bosnians also have had a state with recorded history since the early tenth century; a Byzantine source mentioned a state of Bosnia and its inhabitants who had emerged from Slavic settlements in the territory of the Roman Empire. Originally, the first Bosnian dictionary was written in 1631 by Muhammad Hevai Uskufi while the first Serbian dictionary was written in 1818 by Vuk Sefanović Karađić.[92]

90. Agency for Statistics of Bosnia and Herzegovina. June 2016."Census of population, households and dwellings in Bosnia and Herzegovina, 2013: Final results." Source: http://www.popis2013.ba/popis2013/doc/Popis2013prvoIzdanje.pdf. Retrieved on July 1, 2016.
91. Dnevnik Hr. Source: http://dnevnik.hr/vijesti/svijet/objava-rezultata-popisa-stanovnistva-u-bih-iz-2013-koliko-ima-bosnjaka-srba-i-hrvata---441880.html, Retrieved on July 15, 2016.
92. Muhamed Fazlagić. "Dodik and I Understand Each Other Because We Both Speak Bosnian." BiHbloggen Date 28 June, 2015. Source: https://bosnienbloggen.wordpress.com/2015/06/28/dodik-and-

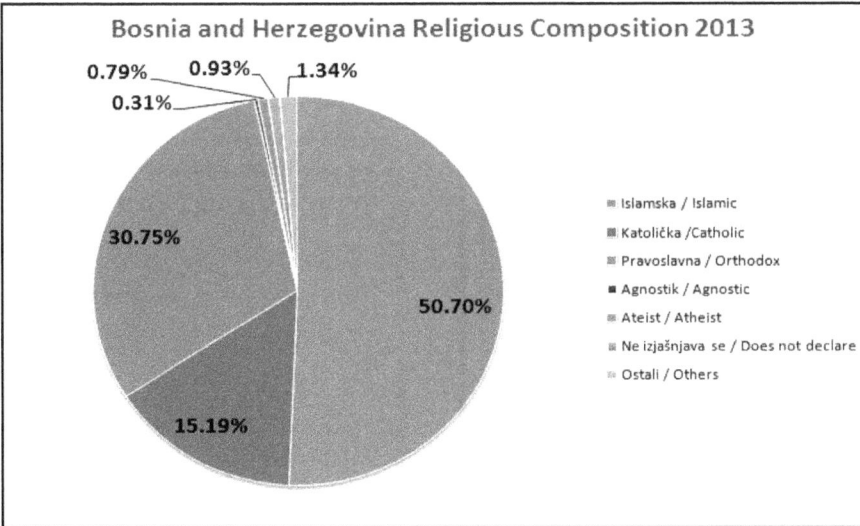

Figure 3.1. Bosnia and Herzegovina Religious Composition 2013 By Jrmcarth-Own work, CC BY-SA 4.0, Source: https://commons.wikimedia.org/w/indexphp?curid=49871411.

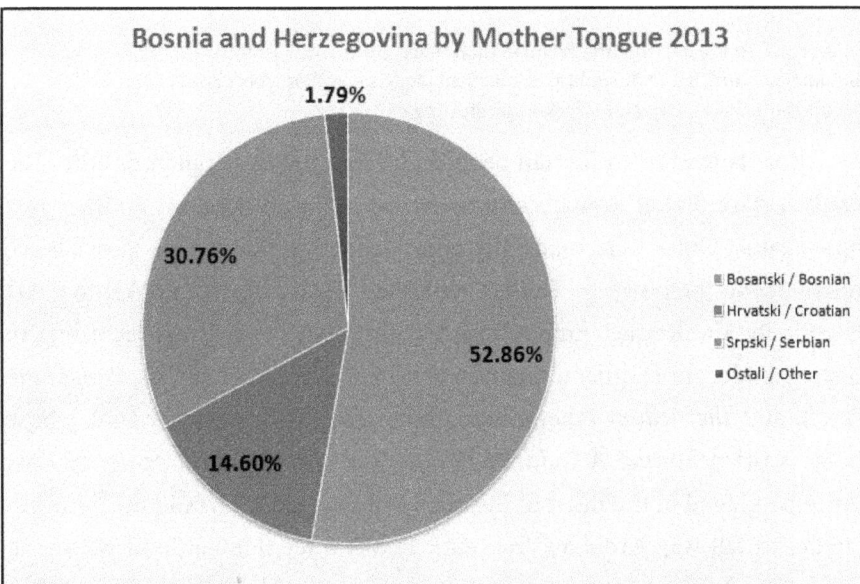

Figure 3.2. Bosnia and Herzegovina by Mother Tongue 2013By Jrmcarth - Own work, CC BY-SA 4.0, Source: https://commons.wikimedia.org/w/index.php?curid=49871648.

In 1995, during the Dayton Peace Accords, the Bosnian language received legitimacy and international recognition. Additionally, the United Nations also recognized the Bosnian language.[93]

Figure: 3.3. To the left, the first Bosnian dictionary, from 1631. To the right, the first Serbian dictionary, from 1818. Source:https://bosnienbloggen.files.wordpress.com/2015/06/rjecnik-bo sanskog-i-rjecnik-srpskog-jezika1.jpg.

Bosnians were an Illyrian people who rejected the Roman Empire. The conflict started after Romans attempted to recruit Illyrians to join them in a fight against Goths - Germans. Illyrians declined recruiting and gave a fierce resistance to the powerful Roman Army for four years, from 6 AD to 9 AD. Eventually, the Roman Empire crushed the Illyrian uprising, recording in history under three different names: *the Great Illyrian Revolt*, *the Pannonian revolt*, and *the Bellum Batonianum*. According to Ivan Lovrenović, whose book is titled *Bosnia: A Cultural History,* the last and most powerful resistance happened in the heart of Bosnian Arduba (today's Vranduk). "The last citadel to fall was Arduba (Vranduk). It was a terrible battle in which, according to Roman historians, the Illyrian women with their children in their

i-understand-each-other-because-we-both-speak-bosnian/.
93. Irene Thompson."Bosnian." Source: http://aboutworldlanguages.com/bosnianUpdated June 13, 2013.

arms threw themselves into the fire when Bato surrendered, rather than be enslaved by the Romans."[94] Nevertheless, the Illyrians were eventually conquered by the Romans and fell under the influence of Christianity.[95]

Ever since the early Middle Ages, Bosnia existed between two great and dominating cultural entities. Lovrenović eloquently pointed out "... it was the Christianity of West and East."[96] He then concludes, "It is also at the root of the multiform cultural parallelism that has characterized Bosnia and Herzegovina throughout history and down to the present day. In the Middle Ages the cultures of east and west coexisted here. Both enriched each other and were themselves enriched but the relics of autochthonous tradition side by side with the Catholic and Orthodox churches – The Bosnia Church. Side by side with the Cyrillic, Greek, Latin and Glagolitic scripts – Bosancica."[97]

The medieval Bosnia, an independent state, reached its high point in the fifteenth century in 1463 when the Ottomans took over, adding further diversity to Bosnian life and traditions.[98] However, even before the Ottoman occupation, Bosnia was sharply divided into three distinctive, hostile, and ecumenical branches of Christianity. The western part of the country belonged to the Roman Catholic Church, whereas the eastern part of the country, along the Drina River, belonged to the Orthodox Church.

In addition to these two already recognized and established branches of Christianity, there was another branch, called Krstjani or "Church of Bosnia", whose followers were called "heretics," and persecuted by the other two branches of Christianity.[99] Consequently, but not surprisingly, the vast majority of "Church of Bosnia" followers embraced Islam from their conquerors in 1463 when the Ottoman Empire conquered Bosnia and introduced a new religion, Islam, to this already complex and religiously hostile region. Furthermore, followers of the Roman Catholic Church converted to Islam, though in very small numbers.

---

94. Lovrenović, ibid., pg, 24.
95. Malcolm, ibid.
96. Lovrenovic, pg. 45.
97. Ibid, pg. 46.
98. Ibid.
99. Senad Agic, Immigration and Assimilation: *The Bosnian Muslim Experience in Chicago*, (Lima, Ohio: Wyndham Hall Press, 2004),pg.14.

Followers of the Orthodox Church, however, converted to Islam on a larger scale for a variety of reasons. None the less, embracing Islam was an "unforgivable sin" that followers of Christianity, especially in the Orthodox Church, were neither willing to forget nor forgive. A sin that Bosnian Muslims have been paying for with their blood since 1878 when the Ottoman Empire left Bosnia and Herzegovina.[100]

Moreover, for over four hundred years, Bosnia and Herzegovina was a significant region of the Ottoman realm. Thus, Bosnia was integrated into the expanding Ottoman Empire. Interestingly enough, Bosnia survived as a distinct administrative unit within the Ottoman Empire. Even though Islam was the official religion under the Ottoman Empire, it was not imposed on other Abrahamic religious followers living in Bosnia. In fact, one of the oldest documents on religious freedom was issued on May 28th, 1463 by Sultan Mehmed II al Fatih, or Mehmed the Conqueror, to Angjeo Zvizdić of the Franciscan Catholic Church located in Fojnica, a small city in Bosnia and Herzegovina.[101] This historical *ferman*, or oath, was a written edict, in which Mehmed al Fatih guaranteed protection of the monks, church and their property. This edict guaranteed tolerance, religious freedom, and rights to all of the non-Muslims living in Bosnia under Ottoman rule.

Furthermore, some Jews who were persecuted by Catholic Inquisitions in Spain, ended up in Bosnia and Herzegovina because the Ottomans guaranteed them religious freedom and provided a safe home in Bosnia.[102] When the Ottoman Empire collapsed on July 13th, 1878, the European powers decided that the Austro-Hungarians would occupy and administrate Bosnia and Herzegovina with the Treaty of Berlin.[103] Bosnia had lived under Ottoman rule and practiced Islam for over 400 years. Not only did Bosnians need to adapt to the new ruling power, Austro-Hungarians, but they also needed to adapt to a new western Christian culture and new administrative language.

---

100. Malcolm.
101. Julianne Hazen, *Contemporary Islamic Sufism in America: The Philosophy and Practices of the Alami Tariqa in Waterport,* (New York. PhD Work, SOAS, University of London, 2011). Source: http://eprints.soas.ac.uk/13816/1/Hazen_3369.pdf.
102. Ibid.
103. Ibid.

Figure 3.4. The original copy of Ahdnama, the 551 year old treaty, has never been taken out of the monastery in the city of Fojnica in Bosnia and Herzegovina. Mehmet II Fatih in 1463 guaranteed the rights of the Bosnian Franciscans. Photo: F. Foćo: source: http://www.avaz.ba.

Figure 3.5. On November 11th, 2015, The President of the Republic of Turkey Recep Tayyip Erdogan received the supreme head of the Catholic church Pope Francis and showed him the famous AHDNAMA document Sultan Mehmet II Fatih issued in 1463 that guaranteed the rights of the Bosnian Franciscans. Photo: Anadolija: source: http://24sata.info.

On June 28th, 1914, on the anniversary of the Battle of Kosovo, "the most sacred day in the mystical calendar of Serban nationalism," when the Ottomans, heavily defeated the Serbian army, Archduke Francis Ferdinand with his wife Sofia visited Sarajevo, capital of Bosnia and Herzegovina and earlier Ottoman territories in the turbulent Balkan region. Bosnia and Herzegovina were annexed by the Austro-Hungarian state in 1908 despite the indignation of Serbian nationalists, who strongly believed that Bosnia should be divided between Serbia and Croatia, where Serbs would obtain the majority of Bosnian territory.[104]

Unfortunately, this was a poorly planned trip and the selection of the anniversary of Battle of Kosovo was a fatal mistake made by the Austrian administration.[105] The date scheduled for Archduke Francis Ferdinand and his wife Sofia to visit Sarajevo was June 28th, which had one more significance. Namely, it was Franz Ferdinand's wedding anniversary. Because Sophie, his beloved wife, was a daughter of a poor Czech aristocrat, she as well as her children were denied royal status in Austria. However, in Bosnia, because of its special status as an annexed territory, it was important to Archduke Ferdinand that Sophie appeared beside him at official proceedings.[106] Serbian nationalist Gavrilo Princip killed Archduke Francis Ferdinand and his wife in Sarajevo on June 28th, 1914.[107]

This tragic event triggered War World I. One month later, Austro-Hungarians declared war against Serbia. The Hapsburgs ruled Bosnia and Herzegovina for four decades ending in 1918.[108] After World War I, Bosnia was included within the newly created kingdom of Yugoslavia and as Dr. Agić concluded, "It was during the first Yugoslavia that Bosnian Muslims began to feel the effects of being pulled between Serbia and Croatia. Bosniaks were denied the right to identify as such and where forced to officially list themselves as either Serb "Muslims" or Croat "Muslims.""[109]

104. Ibid., pg. 155.
105. Ibid., pg.155.
106. International Herlad Tribune." 1914: Archduke Francis Ferdinand Fatally Shot in Sarajevo, June 28, 2014 6:08 am" Archduke Franz Ferdinand assassinated. http://iht-retrospective.blogs. nytimescom/2014/06/28/1914-archduke-francis-ferdinand-fatally-shot-in-sarajevo/?_r=0. Retrieved on November 17, 2016.
107. John A. Garrraty& Peter Gay. *The Columbia History of the World.* (New York: Harper & Row, Publisher, Inc 1972), pg. 981.
108. Ibid., pg. 981.
109. Agić, ibid., pg. 15.

Figure: 3.6. The front page of The New York Herald reporting the assassination of the Archduke Francis Ferdinand in Sarajevo on June 28, 1914.Credit IHT ArchiveSource: http:// iht-retrospective.blogs.nytimes.com/2014/06/28/1914-archduke-francis-ferdinand-fatal-ly-shot-in-sarajevo/?_r=0.

Additionally, Bosnian Muslims lost their country, since the territorial integrity of Bosnia and Herzegovina was compromised and divided between neighboring countries, Serbia and Croatia.[110] After World War II, it became one of the six constituent federal units within the Communist Yugoslavia led by Marshal Tito and during this time, Bosnian Muslims were stripped of their national and religious identity. The Muslim population in the ex-Yugoslavia, based on the last census taken in 1990, was about five million out of the country's twenty-four million total population.

As Dr. Agiċ pointed out, "On the map of old Yugoslavia the Muslims were concentrated in what Serbian nationalists derogatorily refer to as the 'Green belt' running from Bosnia, though the Sandzak and Kosovo, down into Macedonia, merging with Albania. In Belgrade and Zagreb references to this still evoke fears of 'fundamentalist' takeover, initially of the country and eventually of Europe."[111] With the dissolution of the Yugoslav Federation, Bosnia-Herzegovina sought international recognition, which it achieved on April 6th, 1992 following an internationally supervised referendum in which the great majority of its Bosnians voted for independence.[112]

110. Ibid.
111. Ibid., pg. 21.
112. Bosnian Institute. *About Bosnia: History*. Source: http://www.bosnia.org.uk/bosnia/history.cfm retrieved on January 15, 2015.

Subsequently, Bosnia often has been called a *microcosm* of the Balkans, a place where the empires of Rome, Charlemagne, the Ottomans, and the Austro-Hungarians overlapped.[113] This rich and difficult history has led to a genetic diversity uncommon for a country of Bosnia's size. Sarajevo, the capital of Bosnia and Herzegovina, is the only place in Europe where one can find a mosque, a Catholic church, an Orthodox church, and a synagogue within the same neighborhood.[114] It is truly a country unlike any other in Europe, where great powers of the past and the world's great religions overlap and interact.[115] This makes Bosnians inheritors of diverse political, racial, ethnic, religious and imperial traditions. Bosnians came to America with this very complex background, on top of which they added the difficulties of a new language and society. Some even call it European Jerusalem because Muslims, Jews, and Christians, both Orthodox and Catholic, have been co-existing in Bosnia and Herzegovina for centuries.

One of the first Bosnian immigrants who came to Rochester, N.Y, Dr. Asaf Duraković, nicely summed up Bosnian history in his poem titled "Karin Monastery."

Rome, Byzant, Ottomans, Vienna, Budapest
The crowns and the swords
on the bottom of murky waters
Is the same one way road, empty, desolate
Where the glory of the world on its brief path, is walking.[116]

---

113. Malcolm , pg.1.
114. Ibid., pg. 364.
115. Ibid.
116. Julianne Hazen, *Contemporary Islamic Sufism in America: The Philosophy and Practices of the Alami Tariqa in Waterport,* (New York. PhD Work, SOAS, University of London.2011).. Source: http://eprints.soas.ac.uk/13816/1/Hazen_3369.pdf.

Figure: 3.7. Panorama of Sarajevo, Latin Bridge, Sebilj, Emperor's Mosque, Cathedral of the Sacred Heart, Congregational Church/ Source: bs.wikipedia.org

COMPLEX PAST – CURSE OR BLESSING

Despite its sovereign and independent existence ever since the 10th century, Bosnia and Herzegovina has always been under attack and constant pressure from its Orthodox and Roman Catholic neighbors.[117] This punishment especially was acute due to the existence of an autonomous Bosnian Church. This church was a constant target of the Inquisition and its followers were labeled as "heretics."[118] Because of the severe persecution from both Orthodox and the Roman Catholic Church, a majority of them embraced Islam, a new religion brought and introduced to them by the Ottoman Empire in 1463.[119] Furthermore, depending on the time and situation, and because of the threat of crusades and military attacks, Bosnian leaders constantly had to pledge allegiance to the either one church or the other. Despite all odds, Bosnia managed to maintain its sovereignty and territorial integrity until its incorporation into the Ottoman Empire.[120]

Particularly, in the war against Bosnia and Herzegovina and its society, the state of Serbia, Montenegro and Croatia, and their militaristic and paramilitary structures, carried out the genocide against Bosniaks throughout history. There have been ten recorded genocides directed primarily against the Bosnian Muslims, the worst genocide being the most recent, which was a tool for the realization of the national project of Greater Serbia and Greater Croatia.[121] Moreover, Bosnia's neighboring countries, Serbia and Croatia, throughout recorded history, have always looked for the opportunity to divide a sovereign and independent state, Bosnia and Herzegovina, and create a Greater Serbia and Croatia at the expense of Bosnia's territory.

117. Lovrenovic, ibid., pg. 46.
118. Ibid., pg.51.
119. Ibid.
120. Ibid.
121. Agić, ibid.

After the collapse of both the Ottoman (1463-1878) and Austrian-Hungarian (1878-1914) empires and the formation of Yugoslavia as an independent state in 1918, the ethnic tensions between Orthodox Serbian Christians and Roman Catholic Croats erupted, especially during the Second World War. Their mutual goal of a perfect union of South Slavs was finally within their reach in the newly established Yugoslavian state. This proposed union completely ignored Bosnia and its Muslim populations. Nevertheless, nineteenth-century Yugoslavia was heavily dominated by its largest ethnic group, Serbians. Serbia acted as a hegemonic state that exercised a disproportional control over the newly established state. With a Serbian king ruling the Kingdom of Serbs, Croats and Slovenes, and later the Kingdom of Yugoslavia (from 1918 until 1939), Serbia was the dominating power in the first Yugoslavian state, controlling both the army and the political system in the country.[122]

Even though Muslims constituted the third largest ethnic group in the newly established Yugoslavian state, they were never recognized as such. In fact, Serbs and Croats never forgot those Slavs who converted to Islam under Turkish rule, those who left their Orthodox and Roman Catholic religion. They started punishing Muslims by giving them one of three choices: return to their father's orthodox Christian religion, go to Turkey to their new chosen religion, or face death.[123] The exodus of Muslims began during the 19th and 20th centuries, but escalated in the newly established Yugoslavian state, where Serbs had absolute control.

The ultimate goal was to "completely and entirely cleanse Serbia of Muslims" as stated by Noel Malcolm in his book, Bosnia: A Short History. The exodus of Muslims from Serbia started in the last decades of the 19th century and continues through the 21st century. Hundreds of thousands of Muslims migrated to the Ottoman Empire later, in 1923, the Republic of Turkey. The massive exodus of Muslims from Serbia began with the First Serbian Uprising (1804– 1813) against the Ottoman Empire and continued through the collapse of the Ottoman Empire and the Berlin Treaty (1878).

---

122. Ibid., pg. 163.
123. Norman Cigar, *Genocide in Bosnia: The Policy of Ethnic Cleansing.* (Texas A&M University Press. June 1, 2000), pg.17.

Then the exodus remained constant during the establishment of Kingdom of Yugoslavia (1918-1939) and Balkans War (1912-1913) and it escalated during the Second World War (1939-1945) where Serbia implemented a final phase of "ethnic cleansing from Turks."[124]

Figure 3.8. Yugoslavian Muslims fleeing to Turkey, Istanbul 1912.Photo:ByFrederick,Moore‑Source,http://www.damirniksic.com/NG1912.html,PublicDomain,https://commons.wikime‑dia.org/w/index.php?curid=8467591.

Furthermore, when Tito rebuilt Yugoslavia (1945-1989), a Communist Federation, he recognized Bosnia and Herzegovina as one of six equal republics, and acknowledged Muslims of Bosnia and Herzegovina as a distinct nationality. However, Bosnians were not allowed to organize themselves as Bosnians based on the country's name, but around religious identity. During Josip Broz Tito's reign, Bosnians could refer to themselves as Muslims in a national sense which was a synonym of Bosnians.[125] The exodus of Muslims began again, now from Sandžak and Kosovo, Serbia's dominated regions, to Bosnia and Herzegovina. Additionally, the growth in the Muslim population in Bosnia and Herzegovina turned Bosnian Serbs into a minority amid and overwhelming Muslim majority.

124. Ibid., pg. 16,17.
125. Agic, pg. 16.

Despite this fact, Serbia's nationalists dominated in Tito's Yugoslavia as well. Therefore, Serbia continued with its long-term political goal of creating and expanding the ethnically pure Greater Serbia, killing and destroying everyone and everything that reminded them of Turks and Islam.[126] In his book Bosnia: A Short History, Neol Malcolm points out the harsh treatment and massive killings of Bosnian Muslims after World War II. These violent acts were led by the Communist Party, which was dominated by Serbian nationalists. There was a sense of "old scores" being settled at the end of the war.[127] This statement was used by the former Bosnian Serb leader, Radovan Karadzic, who was found guilty of crimes and genocide against humanity during the aggression on Bosnia and Herzegovina between 1992-95. He repeatedly stated that Bosnian Muslims are "vulnerable to marginalization and even to the danger of annihilation by rejecting their true Serbian identity."[128]

The Communist philosophy in Yugoslavia shaped and molded Bosnian religious and cultural identity. Since Communism considered religion a weakness, the practice of Islam was viewed to be shameful and often punishable.[129] As Neol Malcolm rightly asserted,, Islam and Muslims "suffered a double disadvantage in the eyes of the new Yugoslav rulers."[130] One reason for this is that Islam was seen as not only a religion, but also as a way of life.

Additionally, Islam was perceived to be a backward religion; a barrier to progress and prosperity in the newly established communist state.[131] He also wrote about the mass killing and mistreatment of prominent Muslims and intellectuals, whom the Communist Party saw as a possible threats or a competition to their authority. He concluded, "The most severe losses were inflicted by the Communists, at the times, when military units entered villages. All potential opponents, mainly people of higher social standing and intellectuals known to be believers, were simply put to death without any judicial proceedings or investigation."[132]

---

126. Ibid.
127. Malcom, ibid. pg.195.
128. Cigar, pg. 184.
129. Malcom, ibid. pg. 195
130. Ibid.
131. Ibid.
132. Ibid.

Although the majority of the people in Bosnia and Herzegovina identified as Muslim, the political power was in the hands of the Communist Party, which was dominated by Serb nationalists.

Sidreta Fazlić, a Muslim woman, came to America in 1987 after Josip Broz Tito's death on May 4th, 1980, but still during his socialist regimes and long before Serbian attacks on Bosnia and Herzegovina in 1992-1995. She remembers very well how much struggle and injustice she and other Bosnians experienced in the former Yugoslavia. Because her father was a prominent Imam in Bosnia and she was a practicing Muslim, she never joined Communist Party of Yugoslavia (KPJ). Her decision not to fall in line with Communist teaching cost her family dearly and advancement in the work place was impossible. Sidreta Fazlić lived and worked in Sarajevo, and recalls one particular instance that she says she would never forget:

> I was on the list in my company to get a company apartment, which you eventually would buy from the company for a very good price. I was dreaming about the moment to receive the key and have my own place. All my dreams were around that apartment; I was young, enthusiastic and committed to the company. Everybody in the company knew I was the next in line and I deserved that apartment. Unfortunately, my dream never came true. It was Ramadan, the month of fasting, and I was fasting and going to the night prayer to the mosque.
>
> One night I went to one of the city's mosques not knowing that the company had somebody from the Communist Party follow me." It was common practice by the Communist Party to spy on and follow Muslims, especially prominent people and intellectuals. They saw me going to and from the mosque and knew I was also fasting, observing Ramadan. Shortly after that, I was told that I would not get the apartment but those apartments would be granted to the loyal members of Communist Party.

As a practicing Muslim, at that moment I knew that I didn't stand a chance of getting the apartment nor progressing in my company. At that moment, I knew it was time for me to leave my beloved country. My sister already lived in the USA, and she had invited me numerous times to come and visit her. By that time both of my parents were dead and my marriage did not last too long. I was deeply disappointed in my company since my company was everything to me. I left Bosnia and Herzegovina and never looked back. To this day, I have never regretted leaving communist Yugoslavia. I love America and its religious freedom.[133]

Figure: 3.9. Sidreta Fazlić at the Sonnenberg Gardens & Mansion State Historic Park in Canandaigua. August 15, 2015.

133. Sidreta Fazlić. Personal Interview with the author on August 22, 2016.

However, unlike Sidreta Fazlić, who had a strong religious upbringing because of her father's position as an imam, a majority of Bosnian immigrants who came to Rochester did not have deep religious affiliations. In fact, many of them have mixed interfaith marriages and agreed not to practice any religion in their marriage, nor did they want to introduce their children to either religion. This arrangement was possible under Tito's Communist regime that firmly suppressed religion and nationalism. However, after Tito's death and rise of national parties in Yugoslavia, these interfaith marriages were challenged, especially with respect to children's associations with either the fathers' or mothers' religion or nationalities. It is also worth noting here that the high rate of interfaith marriages was a common practice in Bosnia and Herzegovina. Some estimates indicate around forty percent during the reign of the Communist party in former Yugoslavia. Many Muslims who were in interfaith marriages ended up in Rochester, NY.[134]

One of them is Zejto Rastoder, whose life story gives a perfect description of a Muslim living in Tito's Yugoslavia and who was a part of the Yugoslav People's Army. Even though the interview with Zejto is long, it provides the reader with a clear understanding of how Muslims, saw Tito's Yugoslavia and the Yugoslavia People's Army before and during the war. In addition, the interview gives insight into his life in Rochester, NY. Zejto mentioned that he comes from a normal working family with seven siblings— four brothers and three sisters— where the father was the breadwinner and the mother was a stay-at-home mom. Out of seven children, Zejto was earning the best grades in school. At the time, it was very attractive and prestigious to be part of the Yugoslav People's Army. He recalls his childhood: "I wanted to be a religious leader, an Imam, but my father wanted me to be a doctor. Like Buddha's father, he did not want his son to become a spiritualist/an imam. He encouraged me to go to school where I can make some money and have good reputation, especially for the Sandžak region."[135]

He recalls how, at that time, the military academy was the perfect fit for him. People respected the Yugoslav People's Army and anyone could make a

---

134. Hadziosmanović, ibid.
135. Zejto Rastoder, personal interview with author, August 18, 2015.

good living if they were a part of the military. He followed his father's ad-vice, chose to become a military pilot, and went to military school in Mostar, Bosnia and Herzegovina. After finishing military high school, he attended a military academy in the Croatian city of Zadar where he stayed for two years. After two years in Croatia, he came back to Bosnia and specialized in military aviation. Upon finishing his specialization, he was assigned to Zagreb, the capital of Croatia. However, he was not happy with the assignment, since he badly wanted to go to Sarajevo, but he did not have any connection in the military that could pull some strings for him, so he ended up in Zagreb. He concluded, "But it was not that bad, because I met my wife there."[136]

He continued his interview by sharing his struggles, challenges and ex-periences during the war in Bosnia and Herzegovina, his journey to United States and life in Rochester, NY. Soon after he finished the academy and moved to Zagreb, unrest in Yugoslavia was already visible, especially in Slovenia and later Croatia, and signs of end of Yugoslavia as we all knew it were surfacing more visibly. The breakup was inevitable; the only question was whether or not the breakup would be a peaceful and political division or a bloody war as many predicted, especially in Bosnia. Slovenia announced its exit from Yugoslavia and at that moment it was clear that Yugoslavia would be dissolved. Soon after that Croatia announced its exit. Serbia rejected this exit and attacked Croatia with a strong military. As a part of military aviation, Zejto briefly participated in attacks on Slovenia and later on Croatia as a part of the Yugoslav People's Army. Later on, he was assigned to go to city of Banja Luka in Bosnia and Herzegovina. At the beginning of 1992, it was clear to him that the war was going to engulf to Bosnia and Herzegovina and that he would have to attack and kill his own people, Muslims under the umbrella of the Yugoslav People's Army.

Together with other Bosnian Muslims in the Yugoslav People's Military, he decided to leave the military and join a newly established Bosnian Army, called *Patriotska Liga*. At that moment, two-thirds of Bosnian territory were already occupied by the Yugoslav People's Army.

136. Ibíd.

With the helicopters, Zejto further recalls, they were able to transport,mostly wounded soldiers or civilian from Bosnia, region of Bosanka Krajina to Zagreb, the capital of Croatia. There was an air bridge between the two cities of Cazin and Zagreb, which was used to distribute food and medicine to Bosnian population who were under Yugoslavia's military occupation . This air bridge was vital and functioning until the conflict between the self-proclaimed Croatian Republic of Herzeg-Bosnia, supported by Croatia, and the Bosnian Army escalated between 1993 and 1994. Zejto clearly recalls:

> The years 1993 and 1994 were most difficult years for everyone in Bosnia. These were bloody and hungry years for Bosnians. For thirteen months we were eating only soup and bread of soya. There was no flour to make bread, nothing but soy. We found soy in one of the military storage areas and survived because of that. After thirteen months of eating soy for every single meal, United Nations Protection Force (UNPORFOR) started providing some food via their aviations. On top of the regular populations we also had around 60 thousand refugees from other cities to care for. Meanwhile I was assigned to go to Zagreb for further specialization.
>
> Unfortunately, soon after my arrival in Zagreb, the Croatian and Bosnia armies started fighting in Bosnia. Our supervisors in Croatia told us that we needed to leave Croatia as soon as possible. I couldn't go back to Bosnia using the Croatian territory, because they would arrest me. I was hiding in Croatia for some time and it was not easy task. Soon we found out that our friends went to United States and we contacted them. They were living in Rochester, NY and that is how I ended up there. I had never heard of Rochester before the war.
>
> In 1995 we came to Rochester, NY, the same city where we are today, in August 2015, exactly 20 years later. At the beginning we were not organized and I don't know how many Bosnian refugees already were in Rochester, NY in 1995, when I arrived with my wife and my oldest daughter.

In 2007 I wanted to renew my pilot license here in United States, but unfortunately that was out of my reach. Since they asked me to provide them with documentation which I could only obtain from Serbia. I needed to take flying lessons again and pay some forty thousand dollars. At that moment I had around 300 dollars in my pocket. I did however, manage to fly once, on Douglas Helicopter, in Syracuse in 1997 and that made me very happy. Anyway, instead of dream- ing about flying commercial airplanes, I realized that would only be a dream and, I faced the reality and equipped myself to drive buses for the city of Rochester. As a bus driver for the city of Rochester, I drove about a million miles.[137]

Today Bosnia and Herzegovina is a different country. The aggression on Bosnia and Herzegovina between 1992 and 1995 permanently affected and changed Bosnia and Herzegovina and its Muslim populations. Muslim populations of Bosnia and Herzegovina, estimated in 1990, were about 2.4 million out of the country's four and half million and today has been reduced to less than two million.[138] Around 200,000 Muslims were killed between 1992 and 1995 and out of the 200,000 victims in Bosnia, 85% of those were Muslims. Approximately 90% of all war crimes committed in Bosnia were carried out by the Serbian Army (Radovan Karadzic, Ratko Mladic, Arkan and numerous others).[139] Millions of refugees from Bosnia and Herzegovina were displaced inside the country and all around the world. There were approximately 525,038 Bosnian refugees displaced inside Bosnia and 624,250 in other countries.[140] The approximate number of women raped between 1992 and 1995 during the aggression on Bosnia and Herzegovina varies from as low as 12,000 to as high as 60,000, depending on the source and agency.[141]

137. Ibid.
138. Agič, pg. 22.
139. Cigar.
140. Agič, pg 22
141. Maria B. Olujic, *Gendered Violence in Peacetime and Wartime in Croatia and Bosnia-HerzegovinaAt the end of 1992*, (Journal: Medical Anthropology Quarterly: International Journal for the Analysis of Health, March 1998), val 12. Pg: 31-50. The Bosnian government released a figure stating that the number of women who had been raped was about 14,000. Later the same year (in December), the European Community set the number of women of Muslim ethnicity who had been raped by Bosnian Serb soldiers at around 20,000 The Bosnian Ministry of the Interior set the number at around 50,000. It is stated that the European Union (EU) Commission estimated the number of victims at 50,000. At a conference entitled 'Violation of the Human Rights of Women in Bosnia and Herzegovina During the War 1992-1995', held in Sarajevo on 10-11 March 1999, the President of the Organizational Committee, Mirsad Tokaca,

WHO ARE BOSNIAKS?

The term "Bosniak" (Bošnjak) is still confusing even for many modern-day Bosnians.[142] Since many Bosnian Muslims were confused about their religious and national identity, a congress of Muslim intellectuals, in 1993 in Sarajevo, reintroduced the name Bosniak to describe Bosnian Muslims as well as all Muslims living in other parts of former Yugoslavia. The name was reintroduced primarily to diminish the confusing link between religion and national identity. Before the latest census in Bosnia and Herzegovina in 2013, Bosnian intellectuals including politicians, academics, and religious leaders have led a strong and intense campaign to reintroduce the name Bosniaks to the Bosnian Muslim community and have strongly suggested to all Muslims to register themselves as Bosniaks. Therefore, for the purpose of this research paper it is very important for the reader to understand and become familiar with the term 'Bosniak.'[143]

Bosniak is a term by which modern day Bosnian Muslims identify themselves. During the Ottoman Empire all populations of Bosnia were called Bosniak (Bošnjak) regardless of their religion. It is worth mentioning that Christian Bosnians had not described themselves as either Serbs or Croats before the 19th century, specifically before the Austrian occupation in 1878, when the current tri-ethnic reality of Bosnia and Herzegovina was configured based on religious affiliation.[144]

After the fall of the Ottoman Empire and during the Kingdom of Yugoslavia, Bosnian Muslims were completely stripped of the national identity and were

stated that the Commission for Gathering Facts on War Crimes in Bosnia and Herzegovina set the number of raped women between 20,000 and 50,000. Sourse: https://sites.google.com/site/historyofrapeabibliography/author-index/author-index-o/olujic-1998-terror
142. Agić.ibid.pg.119.
143. "Bosniak". Oxford English Dictionary (3rd ed.). Oxford University Press. September Source: https://en.oxforddictionaries.com/definition/us/bosniak retrieved on October 4, 2016.
144. Robert Donia & VA John Fine, *Bosnia and Hercegovina: A Tradition Betrayed*. (Columbia University Press. 2005), pg.72,73, Retrieved 30 October 2012.

only allowed to declare themselves as Serb-Muslims or Croat-Muslims and not as Bosnian Muslims.

Tito, however, again recognized Bosnian Muslims as a distinct nationality and allowed them to organize themselves but only around their religion and not geography.[145] Therefore, Bosnian Muslim was a term that Bosnians used to describe themselves in a national sense. Immediately, after the independence of Bosnia and Herzegovina, Bosnian intellectuals worked tirelessly to affirm usage of the term Bosniak as a synonym for Muslims, a Bosnian population who embraced Islam during the Ottoman Empire, whereas the term Bosnian is used to describe all citizens of Bosnia and Herzegovina regardless of the religion or ethnicity.[146]

Despite this idea from Bosnian political and intellectual leadership to provide an umbrella term which will include all people living in Bosnia regardless of religion or ethnic background and be acceptable for all people living in Bosnia and Herzegovina, Bosnian Serbs and Croats never embraced it.

Figure 3.10. Sarajevo, the capital of Bosnia and Herzegovina and it is rightly called "Jerusalem of Europe "since it is only city in the world that has in a walking proximity: a mosque, synagogue and church. The Gazi Husrev Bey's Mosque, or Bey's Mosque, was built in the center of Baščaršija in 1530. The Synagogue was build in 1581 and the 1889 Roman Catholic Cathedral was built in 1889. Source:http://www.nytimes.com/times-journeys/travel/splintered-pasts-bosnia-herzegovina/.

145. Agič, pg. 119.
146. Ibid, 119.

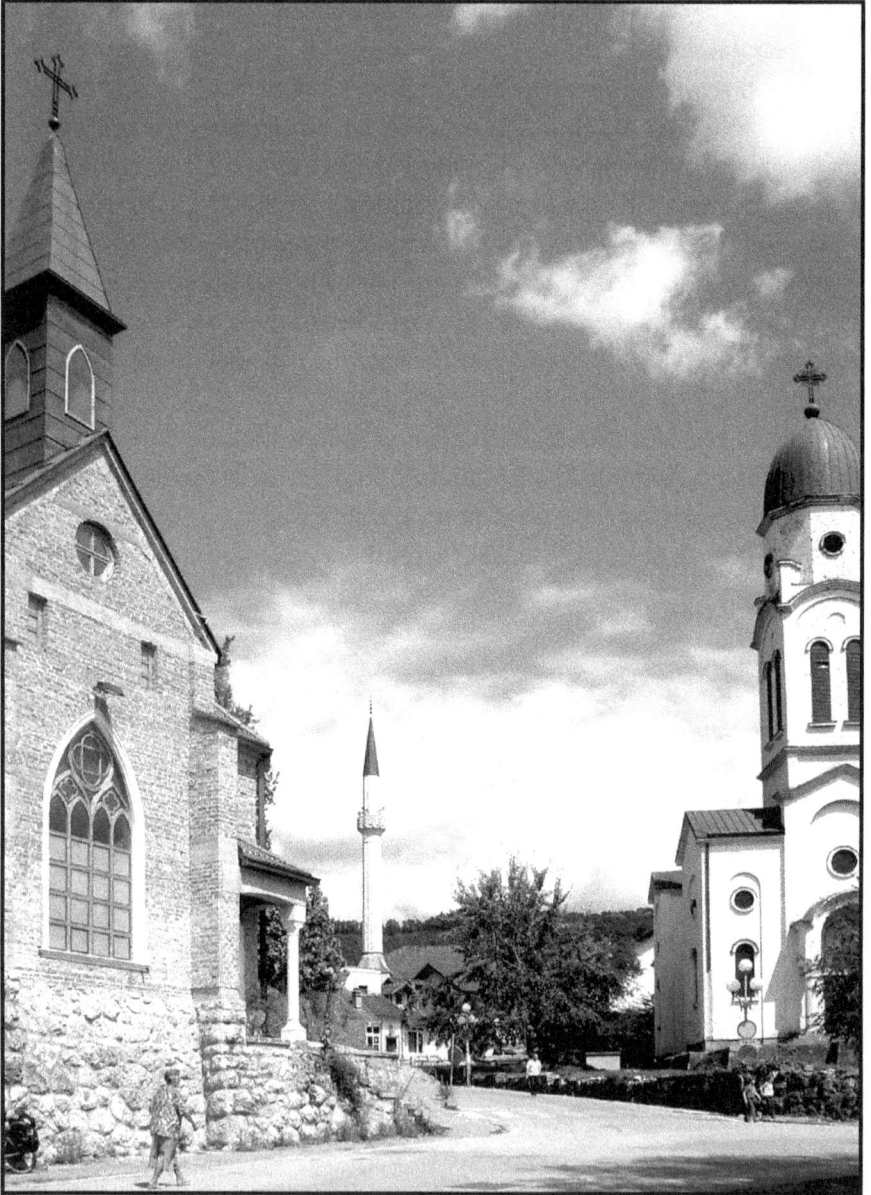

Figure 3.11. Catholic church (left), a Serbian Orthodox church (right), and a mosque (center background) in Bosanska Krupa Source:https://upload.wikimedia.org/wikipedia/commons/8/86/Bosanska_Krupa_Churches.JPG.

CHAPTER FOUR

ROOTS OF BOSNIAN IMMIGRANTS IN AMERICA

According to the immigration center Ellis Island,[147] the first arrivals of Bosniaks to the United States occurred in 1901 with the arrival of Ibra Saradžić from Trebinje in New York.[148] Although there is no clear documentation, it is very likely that some Bosniaks immigrated earlier, from either within Bosnia, or from other countries where they were forced to be by circumstances, either economic or political. Furthermore, during the World Exhibition in 1893 World Columbian Exposition, among the exhibitions from around the world, among them were Bosnians from the Ottoman Empire.[149]

The first Bosnians settled primarily in Chicago seeking better opportunities and better lives in what was perceived as the 'Promised Land'.[150] Bosnians, like many other European immigrants, dreamed of getting rich quickly and returning to their homeland well-established. Sadly, many of them never got rich, nor did they see their homeland ever again.[151] This utopian vision of America did not change much even after one hundred forty years when another group of Bosnians came to America. Halima Stenaklic, a Muslim Bosnian women, who came to Rochester, New York in 1997, describes her vision and her experience of America as follows:

> At first, I was very disappointed in America. I expected America to be like it is in Hollywood. I imagined America to be perfect, everyone rich and wealthy with beautiful houses and roads.

---

147. The State of Liberty-Ellis Island source: www.ellisisland.org, Retrieved on December 26, 2016.
148. Faruk Bogučanin, "*Četri Bošnjaka Potonula sa Titanikom*" Bosnjaci Net.Source: http://bosnjaci.net/prilog.php?pid=22974, May 24, 2006
149. Ibid.
150. Ibid
151. Ibid.

Muhamed Jaganjac immigrated to Chicago from Okoliste in March 1907 with two relatives, one of whom went on to establish the Bosnian community in Montana. Here Jaganjac stands wearing a fez cap and a fancy moustache, common among Bosnian Muslim men at the time. (Courtesy of Zerina Zvizdic.)

Figure 4.1. Muhamed Jagajac: Immigrated to Chicago from Okolište in March 1907. Here Jaganjac stands wearing a fes cap and fancy moustache, common among Bosnian Muslims man at the time.Source: Samira Puskar. Bosnian Americans of Chicagoland. (Chicago, Arcadia Publish, 2007),pg. 25.

I also thought that other Bosnian refugees were already established, rich and had beautiful houses and jobs. Unfortunately, nothing was farther from the truth. When I arrived in Rochester, New York, the America I thought was nothing like I imaged. My sponsors, my brother-in-law with his family, were living in an apartment in a very poor area. They had enough to survive, but nothing more. My husband, my eleven- month-old baby and I had to move into our apartment in forty-five days. We did not have anything in which to live; not a spoon, not a bed, not a table, nothing – period. I was told that we would have to go throughout neighboring streets at night and look for some furniture, hoping that somebody had thrown something out during the day before garbage collection comes through their streets. That definitely was the hardest thing to swallow.

I could not imagine that I would have to sleep with my baby on somebody's thrown-out bed. I started crying and crying because even during the war in Bosnia I did not go to look for somebody's garbage and now I had to do exactly that in wealthy America. That was a cold reality for me that made me realize there are two cultures in America: one for rich people and one for poor people. Nevertheless, we survived during that period, which was part of our lives, our path.Because I was young, everybody told me to go to school and college, but I did not listen. I needed money since we came from the war and I did not see money for a long time. Also, my daughter was on my mind. I was afraid that I wouldn't be able to give her food and clothes if I went to school.

I prayed very hard and asked God to help me to find a job where I can make some money for me and my daughter. After five months I started working and I made 5 dollars and fifty cents per hour. I received weekly checks which couldn't cover my bills. Soon I found a second job just to be able to pay bills and survive in America. On top of all these struggles, my heart and my mind were constantly on Bosnia. I prayed to God every night to help me make enough money to buy a ticket for me and my daughter to permanently return to Bosnia and Herzegovina. I knew that my husband wouldn't go back since he came here determined to succeed, but I saved every penny that I could for the ticket. In Bosnia I had my family: my mother, father, sister and two brothers. Sadly, my mother passed away and my plans changed. From that moment, I did not want to permanently move to Bosnia but was determined to make some money and help my family in Bosnia.[152]

However, during the nineties, approximately 350,000 Bosnian immigrants came to the United States because of the Balkan war.[153] In fact, refugees from Bosnia and Herzegovina were the largest single group to be admitted to the United States during that time period.[154] Dr. Senad Agić, a prominent Bosnian Imam and Muslim community leader in the United States, who resides in Chicago, explored the various aspects of the Bosnian Muslim community in America.

152. Stenaklić, ibid.
153. Agić, Ibid.
154. Kathleen Newland, *Impact of U.S. Refugee Policies on U.S. Foreign Policy* (New York: The American Assembly, 1995).

In his book entitled *Immigration & Assimilation* he emphasizes a complex background of Bosnian Muslims, a very distinctive European group with Islamic faith but European roots and well-blended Christian and Islamic culture. He points out various effects that assimilation has had on this culture.[155] He concluded that the first group of Bosnian immigrants was a small and uneducated group, unprepared to preserve their cultural and religious identity. They came to the United States and began working in low-skilled labor jobs, usually in mines, working long hours in the low-paid jobs.[156] However, as Halima pointed out in her interview, this fact did not change much even for some Bosnian refugees who came to America during and after the war. They also had to work long hours in minimum wage jobs.

In addition, Agić argues that Bosnian Muslims began immigrating to the United States in significant numbers in the late 19th century, usually single, young men without formal education or plans to stay permanently in the United States. Furthermore, Bosnian Muslims avoided permanent links and ties to the United States. Most of them stayed single and never purchased land or learned English. Because most of these immigrants never returned home, they were buried in Islamic cemeteries in the United States. On the other hand, the Bosnian refugees from the nineties were a completely different group of immigrants. They were a much larger group than the immigrants from the 19th century were. Many came with their families, which gave them an established support system. They were also better educated, and they quickly learned the necessary tools to be self-sufficient. Many refugees came with degrees and already spoke some English, which gave them the opportunity to find jobs and go to school. They started organizing themselves, first through religious and then cultural and political organizations.[157]

Similarly, historian John Powell, in his book entitled Encyclopedia of North American Immigration, confirms that Bosnians began to arrive in North America around 1900. Their numbers, however, remained small until the flood of refugees from the dissolution of Yugoslavia in the early 1990s.

---

155. Agić.
156. Agić.
157. Agić.

Arif Dilich, seated bottom left, takes a photograph with 50 or so of his fellow Bosnian American workers, employed by the Paschen Construction Company, in 1923. (Courtesy of the Bosnian-American Cultural Association.)

Figure 4.2. Arif Dilich, a Bosnian Immigrant and successful businessman with Bosnians workers.

Powell also emphasizes that the Bosnian-American community in the United States are more than 100 years old.[158] Bosnians usually worked as manual laborers, uneducated and unequipped to do other well-paid jobs. He concludes that Bosnian immigrants, alongside other European immigrants, helped build America's cities and its economy while dreaming of returning to Bosnia.[159] According to the available documentation, the Titanic most likely contained four Bosniaks originating from Badica. Their names were Ejdo Rekić (38), Reggio Delalić (25), Ćerim Balkić (26) and Hussein Sivić (40). Tickets for this trip were purchased in Switzerland, and they boarded as third-class passengers in Southampton, England.

158. John Powell, *Encyclopedia Of North American Immigration*. (New York: Infobase Publishing, 2009).
159. Ibid.

The *Titanic* transported four Bosnians en route to America. The passengers, hailing from northwest Bosnia, had third-class cabins. As the story goes, the *Titanic* sank after hitting an iceberg in North Atlantic waters in 1912, bringing the immigrants down with it. They were reportedly trying to reach Harrisburg, Pennsylvania, in search of a small Bosnian community and a steady amount of work in the mines.

Figure 4.3. Source: Bosnian Americans of Chicagoland by By Samira Puškar, pg 18.

Their final destination was Harrisburg, Pennsylvania. Some of them, such as Ejdo Rekić, had already been to America.[160] As is known, the Titanic struck an iceberg on April 14, 1912, just before midnight, and would have sunk two and a half hours later the next morning. In addition to the surviving passengers, a number of bodies from the sea were recovered and buried in Halifax, Canada. So, although it is unlikely, there is a possibility that the remains of some Bosniaks are buried in Halifax. To my knowledge, although it was known earlier that there were people from the former Yugoslavia on the Titanic, there never was an organized effort to bring together and thoroughly examine the list of tragic deaths of passengers from the area. Therefore, because of the lack of thorough documentation the details remain unknown. Also, a few Croatian immigrants survived the sinking of the Titanic.

It is important to add that a second wave of Bosnian immigrants arrived in the United States after the end of World War II in 1945, when Bosnia and Herzegovina was integrated as a region within the newly established communist country of Yugoslavia, led by Josip Broz Tito. Bosnian Muslims went through political changes again and many of them were forced to look for a better future outside their home country.

160. Samira Puskar, *Bosnian Americans of Chicagoland* (Chicago, Arcadia Publishing, 2000),pg. 18.

Some of them had to leave Bosnia to save their lives because they sided with Germany and Italy and fought against Tito's Communist forces, while others were opposed to the religious repression instigated by the Communist Party.[161] Again, when Tito lifted travel restrictions in the 1960s, many Bosnian Muslims left the country, especially Bosnians with formal education, including teachers, engineers, and students. A majority of them came with their families determined to make the United States their new home.[162]

---

161. Powell, ibid.
162. Ibid.

GENERATIONAL GAP AMONG BOSNIAN IMMIGRANTS

B osnian immigrants persistently organized themselves through their religious and cultural organizations to preserve their religion, culture and language. However, they faced challenges with their children and grandchildren who were born and raised in the United States. Second- and third-generation Bosnian Americans showed the most divergence from Bosnian culture.[163] While the parents and community's elders emphasized and encouraged the use of Bosnian language and marriage within the community to preserve their identity, their children and grandchildren branched out beyond the Bosnian community. This brought conflict not only in homes, but also in the Bosnian communities. The generational gap between Bosnian immigrants was clear. Bosnian community leaders did not feel comfortable passing the torch of preserving Bosnian identity to the younger generation. More and more Bosnians from the second and third generations began dating Americans, rather than marrying other Bosnians.[164]

Unlike the first groups of Bosnians who came earlier, the refugees from Bosnia who arrived during the Balkan War benefited from the Bosnians who were there before them because the second group of Bosnian immigrants managed to organize themselves and establish community centers, clubs, coffeehouses. This made the transition for the new Bosnian refugees easier.[165] As stated earlier, the immigration wave in 1945 consisted mostly of families planning to make the United States their new home. Therefore, they learned English, went to school, bought homes, opened businesses, and emphasized education for their children. Subsequently, this expanded their outreach and they became involved outside their own community.

---

163. Agić.
164. Powel.
165. Ibid.

They also started interfaith dialogue. As a result, the first Bosnian Mosque was established under the leadership of a Bosnian Imam and leader, Camil Avdić, in Chicago, in 1957.[166] He also wrote a pioneering book, *Outline of Islam*, for Muslim-American children.[167]

---

166. Agić, ibid.
167. Agić, Ibid.

BOSNIAN REFUGEES IN AMERICA – BACKGROUND

T he refugees experience differs drastically from that of immigrants. Immigrants usually choose to leave their home country and move to another country looking and hoping for better economic, political, social opportunities, whereas refugees are forced to leave their home in fear of persecution, war, or violence. Serbian Military aggression in Bosnia and Herzegovina lasted from 1992 to 1995; it displaced more than 2 million people, and of these around half a million left Bosnia and fled to other countries.[168] At the beginning of the Serbian aggression, many Bosnians found temporary refuge in neighboring Croatia. A majority of them were hoping to move to other European countries, primarily Germany. They were eventually granted temporary asylum in Germany and some other European countries. Unfortunately for Bosnian refugees, primarily those who resided in Germany, were pressured to move on, either returning to Bosnia or permanently resettling in overseas countries such as the United States, Canada, Australia, and New Zealand.[169]

These Bosnians were faced with two hard choices. First, they could return to Bosnia and Herzegovina, a country torn apart by war, and without job perspective in their future. Sadly, many would not have a home to return to and they would be refugees in their own country. Their second choice was to go overseas and permanently resettle. All Bosnian refugees who were admitted to enter the United States, Canada, Australia or New Zealand chose to permanently move and start a new life in one of these countries listed above. Many refugees from Bosnia and Herzegovina decided to make the United States their new home settling in cities such as St. Louis, Chicago,

168. Catherine Phuong, "Freely to Return: Reversing Ethnic Cleansing in Bosnia-Herzegovina "(Journal of Refugee Studies, 2000), Vol.13, No.2
169. Ibid.

Jacksonville, Grand Rapids, Bowling Green, Salt Lake City, New York City, Los Angeles, and Dallas.[170] Additionally, large Bosnian communities are found in Boston, Boise, Charlotte, Cedar Rapids, Waterloo, Des Moines, Denver, Detroit, Nashville, Milwaukee, Phoenix, Portland, Seattle, Utica, Rochester, Indianapolis, Fort Wayne, Atlanta, Louisville, and Hartford.[171]

Under the leadership of President Bill Clinton and his Democratic party, the United States granted Bosnians refugee status and provided them with temporary governmental assistance. From early 1990 until 2000, there were around 100,000 Bosnians living in the United States.[172] This was the first time since the aftermath of the Second World War, when a massive outflow of refugees came from Europe to the United States. The United States government immediately gave Bosnian refugees Social Security numbers that allowed them to work. Additionally, through government assistance, they also were able to learn English and receive job training. Amela Bodulović, a Bosnian woman who came to Rochester, NY on December 10, 1993 said "We are so thankful to our president Bill Clinton who allowed us to come to the United States and established many programs for Bosnian refugees, and gave us opportunity to learn English and new skills, work and a fresh start to a new life. If he did not allow us to come here, who knows what would have happened to us and where we would have ended up."[173]

Even though the United States, under President Bill Clinton, accepted many Bosnian refugees, the United States failed to intervene and prevent the bloodshed and suffering of the Bosnian people. Because of this pacifistic policy, three mid-level State Department officials resigned, saying they could not continue to acknowledge Serbian aggression and do nothing. One of these officials is Jon Western, who, for almost a year, received information and images on his desk that he could not ignore. One of them showed a 9-year-old Muslim girl, who had been raped for two days by Serbian fighters before she died, while her parents were forced to watch. "This was pretty indicative of the type of things we were getting on a daily basis,"[174]

170. Agić.
171. Agić.
172. Ibid.
173. Amela Bodulović, e-mail message to author, November 27, 2014.
174. Steven A. Holmes, State Dept. Balkan Aides Explain Why They Quit, August 26, 1993. source: http://www.nytimes.com/1993/08/26/world/state-dept-balkan-aides-explain-why-they-quit.html, Retrieved on December 29, 2016.

State Dept. Balkan Aides Explain Why They Quit

By STEVEN A. HOLMES

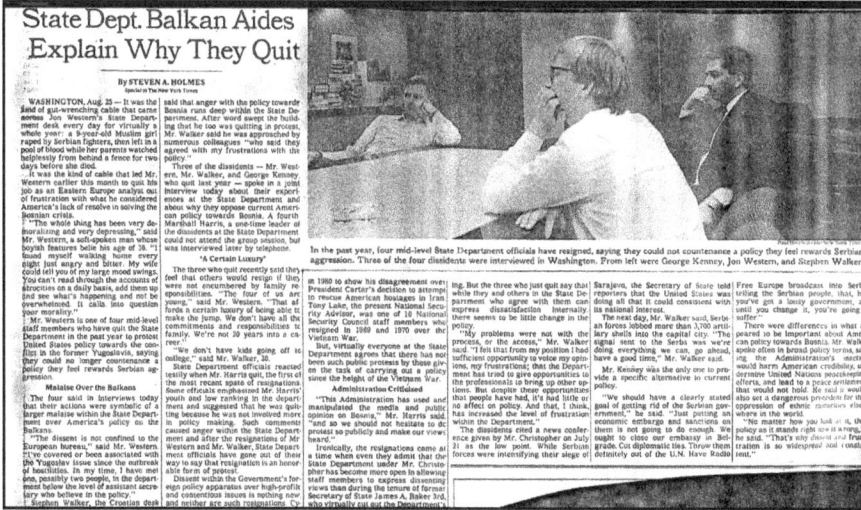

Figure 4.4. From left were George Kenney, Jon Western, and Stephen Walker. (Paul Hosefros/ The New York Times) source: http://archives.ubalt.edu/hdb/pdf/b-117-19_vii_19.pdf.

Mr. Western said. Such devastating information led Mr. Western, along with Mr. George Kenney, and Mr. Stephen Walker, to quit their jobs. Indeed, the United States as well as the United Nations could have done much more to prevent the genocide in Bosnia and Herzegovina. The testimony of Bosnian refugee, who came to Rochester, NY in September 1995 and does not want to disclose her identify, captured the difficulties and challenges which Bosnian refugees had to endure through their journey from Bosnia to the United States.

> I came to Rochester, NY in September 1995. I lived in Germany from 1992-1995 with my parents. When I came to Rochester, I joined my husband and his parents. We all lived together and rented a house from an elderly woman. Beginning was hard. Coming to a new country not knowing a language, being so far away from a family did not make things any easier. So here, we are to start all over again. First, I enrolled in ESL[175] classes in the morning and Child Care classes in the afternoon.

---

175. ESL: English as a second language: the study of English by nonnative speakers in an English-speaking environment.

After a year of going to school learning English and receiving my CDA[176] diploma, I started working. At the same time, we started our family and our first child was born in 1997! My in-laws took care of my son while my husband and I continued to work. After a few years, we purchased our first house and became parents two more times! We proudly named our children with traditional Bosnian names and try to visit my family in Bosnia as much as we could. I miss my old friends, my mom, dad, brother, cousins...especially when it comes to holiday time and families getting together.

I miss our tight knit communities where everybody drinks coffee together and are invited to each other houses and actually you know your neighbors ...while here all my neighbors want their privacy and "Good morning" is the closest you get to people that live next door to you. I miss pedestrian streets with no traffic, getting fresh bread in the morning from the bakery for breakfast, and listening to people talk to each other and seeing familiar faces. I miss all of that and much, much more. Here in Rochester we live in suburb of West Irondequoit and we can proudly say that we are happy with our lives here. There are many differences between Bosnia and America, there is always going to be likes and dislikes. We were given our second chance to life after we escaped genocide in Bosnia and definitely with hard work we accomplished a lot. There is always going to be a question, "What if I didn't come here and is there another place where I would be happier "? I still think once you are taken from your roots and your homeland it doesn't matter where you are...but I do wish I were closer to my homeland!![177]

Earlier Bosnian immigrants, or Bosnian Americans, as well as Muslim Americans from a variety of ethnic backgrounds, generously responded to the refugee crisis. They regularly organized help through their mosques or cultural clubs and soon philanthropy directed toward Bosnian refugees became central to Muslim-American life.[178]

176. CDA,The Child Development Associate (CDA) Credential.
177. Anonymous. E-mail message to author, November 26, 2014.
178. Agic.

Additionally, many non-Muslim Americans went out of their way to help Bosnian refugees. Until the early 1990s, most Americans did not even know Europe had a Muslim population or where Bosnia was located.[179] One of them is Patricia Reed, a Rochester native who remembers very well when she met her neighbor after living across the street from him for ten long years. This opportunity came with the grand opening of a new restaurant in the neighborhood where she met her Bosnian neighbor. "This was the beginning of what I would call my new life," she said.

Frank told Patricia his last name was Nadz and that he had immigrated to Canada at the age of 17. As a young boy, together with other older Croats, he left Croatia and former Yugoslavia to save his life. After World War II, many Croats and Muslims left Yugoslavia because they feared for their lives since the Communist Party was killing everyone who sided with the Nazis or was religious and influential. Frank left his family, went to Austria then to Germany, and finally settled in Canada for a while. In Canada he worked for a construction company, but subsequently company moved to the United States, to New York State. Frank finally came to Rochester in 1964 where he still resides. Two sisters, Nina and Jasna, also from former Yugoslavia, and who came to Rochester during the seventies, were gearing up to help Bosnian refugees who were about to arrive in Rochester.

Frank and his friends helped Bosnian refugees in processing their paper work, interpreting and driving them to help them get settled. Patricia concludes, "Looking back, it seemed somewhat curious that I had just met Frank after living across the street from him for 10 years. Little did I know that I was about to embark on a new journey in my life that would result in me getting quite an unconventional education and making some of the best friends in my life to date!" She recalls their regular conversations, after their initial meeting at the local restaurant.

---

179. ibid., pg. 87.

Figure 4.5. Patricia Reed. Rochester native who went out of her way to help Bosnian Refugees in Rochester, NY.

One day about the end of September 1993, he told me he had been very busy. He told me about the contact he had with Nina and Jasna and how he was helping with some Bosnians. At that time, I wasn't into watching the television news, and I had no idea where Bosnia was! Frank proceeded to tell me that this young guy had been in prison and was now here in Rochester as a refugee from Bosnia. PRISON !! I wondered what in the world this guy had done and how was it that he had been released and sent to America! It didn't take too long to figure out that he had been a prisoner of war and with the help of the American Red Cross, came to America as a refugee. He arrived in Rochester on September 15, 1993. The very first to arrive in Rochester. Others came the next day. Frank soon introduced me to Hasan, sometime in the early winter. I was totally fascinated with the fact that we communicated quite well without either of us speaking the others' language.

We drew pictures of objects that we were trying to identify in each language, thus beginning to learn words foreign to both of us. I believe the first word I learned was "riba", meaning fish. I spent as much of my free time as possible learning about the state of affairs in Yugoslavia, and how it was now broken up into other countries. I found out about the war, and basically how peoples' lives were being turned upside down. Genocide, and the fact that it was going on at the end of the 20th century, was something that was hard to fathom.

I wanted to soak up everything that I possibly could about Bosnia. I wanted to learn about the Muslim religion and the culture and the language. I wanted to help these people...and so it began.[180]

However, despite government assistance and that offered by religious and humanitarian organizations as well as private citizens, many Bosnians had a hard time adjusting from their prior, usually very simple life, to a complex life in the United States. Refija Kapic from Kamenica, who has been living in Rochester for the last twenty years, remembers the first time when she came to Rochester in early 1994.

Every day I was crying and for a long time, I felt homesick and could not adjust to the new environment.Even though I appreciated help we received from the Government, such as food stamps and health insurance, it did not feel right to me to take money and live without working that was not "halal"[181] for my family and me. After two months, one day while in school in Chili, Rosen, from Catholic Family Center, came to our class and said that she found a job for two people.
After some body translated that, I immediately raised my hand and said that both my husband and I want to work. The next day we started working at a hotel, but we did not understand anything so our daughter who had picked up some English was coming with us to work and translating for us and for our supervisor.
    I was determined and worked very hard to do my job successfully. We worked over eighty hours a week and worked every day, seven days a week. We managed to save enough money to buy our first home on Lake Avenue, without taking out a mortgage[182] and with some help from our kids in only three years. Meanwhile I was helping my family in Bosnia. Now both of my sons have their business. My older son is in retail and the younger one runs a restaurant. I am so thankful to God that neither of my sons is drinking alcohol, they are practicing their religion, and they send their kids to our mosque.[183]

---

180. Patricia Reed, personal interview with author, October 2014.
181. Halal Definition: denoting or relating to meat prepared as prescribed by Muslim law.
182. Conservative Muslims do not want to pay or receive interest.
183. Refija Kapić, telephone interview with author, December 03, 2014.

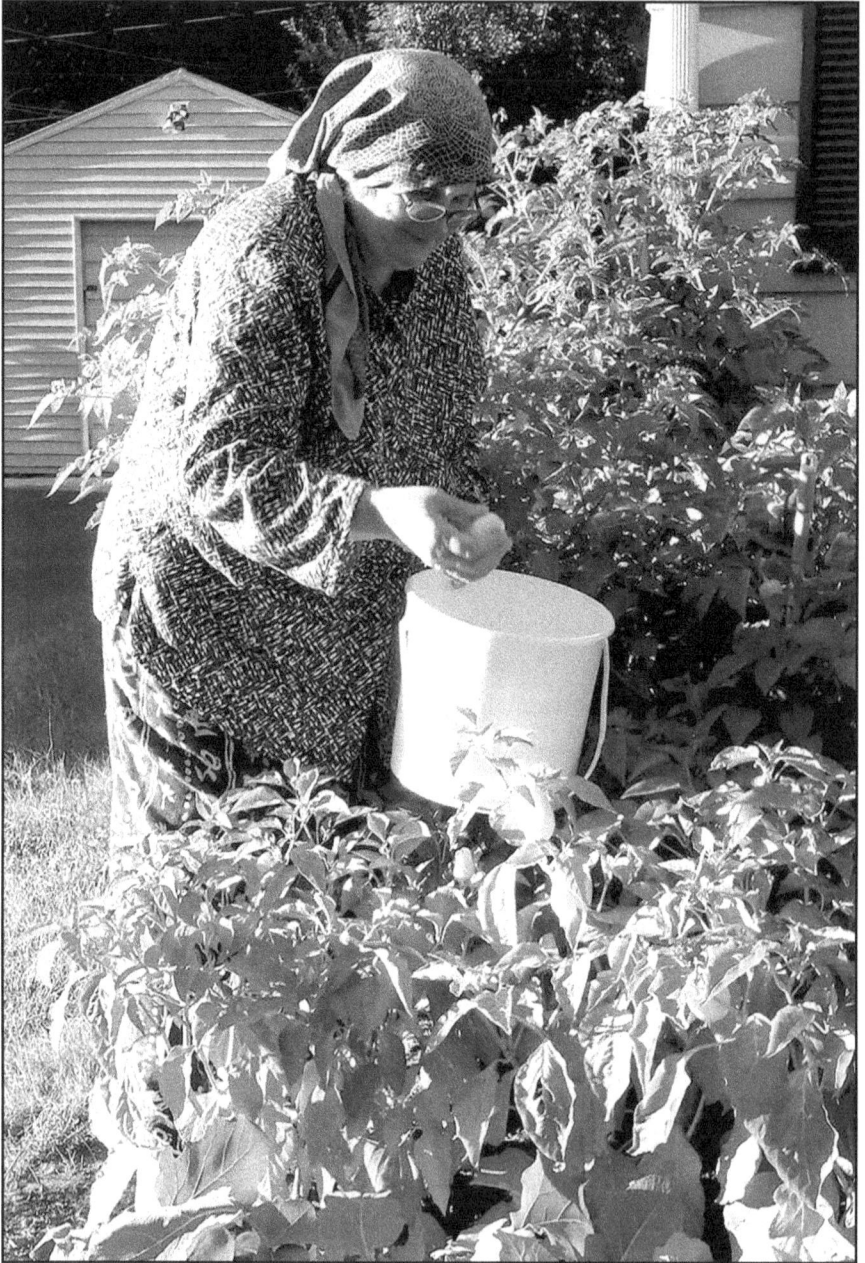

Figure 4.6. Rafija Kapić in her garden growing peppers in front of her home in Rochester, NY September 1, 2016.

CHAPTER FIVE

BOSNIAN REFUGEES
IN ROCHESTER

Bosnian refugees came to Rochester in two major waves. The first group was comprised mostly of prisoners from concentration camps run by Bosnian Serbs and Croats. The second group was made up of wounded soldiers, couples from interfaith marriages, widows with children, Bosnians whose homes were destroyed or under Serbian occupation, mentally or physically disabled persons, and women at risk. Many refugees from Srebrenica ended up in Rochester as well as Bosnians who were victims of torture and systematic acts of violence. This group came directly from Bosnia and Herzegovina starting in 1993, never having lived anywhere but Bosnia. They came directly from the warzone, seeking basic human needs: food, shelter, medicine. Sabiha Mahmutović, one of the first comers, came to Rochester in 1994 with two sons. About her journey from Bosnia to America, she says the following.

> My sister-in-law sent me a letter from Rochester where she mentioned that she went to *Mevlud*[184] and asked me to come with my children to Rochester. The knowledge that I would be able to go to the mosque in America made me very happy and I immediately agreed to come to Rochester. However, when we arrived in Rochester there was no Bosnian mosque or religious organization/dzemat. Later on in 1995, there was a Bosnian Cultural Club where our Bosniaks gathered, but there was no congregation or any religious organization for Bosnians. The Pakistani community helped us a lot. Especially women named Ruhi. She was very active in helping Bosnian refugees. She even brought us packages as a surprise.

---

184. *Mevlud* or *Mewlid* (Prophet Muhamed's Birthday); in Bosnia, however, mostly all traditional religious gatherings are called Mevlud.

She led us to a mosque but it was an Ahmediyya mosque and we did not feel comfortable going there. Soon we find out about the Turkish mosque and we started to go to there. Unfortunately, soon a divide formed among the Turks.

One group wanted to use space in the mosque for consuming alcohol, playing chess, etc. The other group insisted that the building should strictly be used for religious purposes and opposed the use of alcohol. It came to a division forming two groups. Imam Mehmet Aktas with a group of Turks managed to buy a new building and they were soon joined by Bosniaks. More and more Bosnians began to come to the Friday prayers and *Teravija*, night prayer during the month of Ramadan, but still there was no organization of Bosniaks on the religious level. All religious needs of the Bosniaks took place in the Turkish mosque led by Imam Mehmed.[185]

The second wave of Bosnian refugees started coming in 1998 from European countries, primarily Austria and Germany. These refugees were given the option of either returning to Bosnia or moving to Canada, Australia, or America. Many chose one of the three countries instead to returning to Bosnia and Herzegovina. Those who settled in Rochester, NY got there primarily because they had relatives already living in this city. For this group, adjustment was much easier because they had entered a new country once before. They already had skills to aid in adjustment and self-efficiency. Nevertheless, many of these new immigrants had doubts, questioning if their decision to come to America had been the right choice. This group played a pivotal role in organizing the Bosnian community in religious aspects.

It appears, however, that the first known Bosniak (Bošnjak) immigrant who came to Rochester was Dr. Asaf Duraković MD, PhD, DSc, FACP, professor of Nuclear Medicine and Radiology, a specialist in all aspects of nuclear and radiation medicine. In 1968 Dr. Duraković immigrated to Canada and attended McMasters University in Hamilton.

---

185. Sabiha Mahmutović, personal interview with author on August 15, 2015.

He completed his residency in Nuclear Medicine at University of Rochester/Strong Memorial Hospital. Professor Duraković was the first one to organize regular Jummah prayers at Interfaith Chapel of the University of Rochester. He also served as a first Imam who led the Jummah during Friday prayer, and organized the First Teravih Salat (extra nightly prayers) during Ramadan. According to Dr. Malik Salahuddin, history professor at SUNY Brockport, who knew and worked with Dr. Duraković:

> Sheikh Asaf was the most educated man whom I have met in my life. He has an unbelievably good memory and he was a good public speaker. With his strong Islamic faith and courage, he reenergized all of us, the first group of Muslims who lived in Rochester. He organized our prayers at the University of Rochester and he led our prayers. He was our first Imam. He is the only man that I know who would choke up and cry when talking about our beloved Prophet. The tears would simply run from his eyes, whenever he was talking about our Prophet. However, he did not stay in Rochester long; he moved on to Washington. He was also a Sufi with a very large number of followers of American converts to Islam. Ninety-five percent of them where highly educated white professionals.[186]

Besides Dr. Duraković, there were two other immigrants from Bosnia and Herzegovina residing in Rochester, sisters named Nina and Jasna Ibrahimović, who came to America with their mother in the early seventies. Their mother is from Istra, Italy, but their father was from Tuzla, Bosnia. These two sisters helped the first wave of Bosnian refugees.[187] They acted as translators and drove them to places like the grocery store, social services, and doctors' offices; they were available to Bosnian immigrants anytime they were needed. According to Patricia Reed, the American native who helped Bosnian refugees and still does: "Nina and Jasna or Jashi, as the Bosnians used to call her, were the welcoming committee and had been here about as long as Franjo Nadz."[188]

186. Dr. Salahuddin Malik , personal interview with author, October , 2015 and September 2016.
187. Mediha Bećirović, personal interview with author, December 3, 2014.
188. Reed, ibid.

Figure 5.1. Dr. Asaf Durakovic Sunny Miller interviews on depleted uranium in London. The BBC reported on his alert about high uranium levels in civilians exposed to US bombing in Afghanistan (photo ©2003 Charlie Jenks) May 19th, 2003 source:http://www.grassrootspeace. org/depleted_uranium.html.

Figure 5.2. Dr. Salahuddin Malik addressing the Bosnian Co munity in Rochester at the Bosnian Culture Center during one of the community's events. June 6th, 2015.

Figure 5.3. Ismeta Jusić with her husband Enis Jusic during our interview at her home in Rochester, New York. August 25th, 2015.

Additionally, Ismeta Jusić, a Bosnian woman who came to Rochester among the first refugees, also talked about Nina and Jasna, sharing stories that described how much they helped her and her family as well as many other Bosnian refugees. Ismeta said, "They worked tirelessly bringing Bosnian refugees food, clothing and furniture. Sometimes, I felt sorry for the sisters who gave their time and money for us. They would even bring furniture for us with their car or would find an American friend who would deliver furniture for us. I respect and appreciate them. They deserve recognition and a big thank you from our Bosnian community."[189] Despite my efforts to reach these women who helped the first Bosnian refugees in Rochester, New York, I was not able to get an interview with them.

There were other people from the former Yugoslavia who lived in Rochester and helped newcomers, among them were Zvonko Matana, Margita Amidzic, and Lena Horwath. Another woman who devoted an extraordinary amount of time to help the Bosnian refugees was Patricia Reed. She sacrificed her personal life, time and money to help people in need. In the abovementioned interviews, she speaks from personal experience having worked with Bosnian refugees for a long time.

---

189. Ismeta Jusić, personal interview with author August 23, 2015.

Likewise, Fatima Fazlić, better known to the Bosnian Rochester community as *Fatima Prevodilac* (Fatima Translator) came to the United States in 1978 and eventually ended up in Rochester, with her two daughters and sister. She served the Bosnian community in Rochester ever since she moved to the city. Here is how she summed up her journey from Bosnia to Rochester,:

> I arrived at New York City in February 1978 from Sarajevo, after my childhood friend sponsored me on a three-month visit. It was a time when there were no political tension in Bosnia and a time when there were hardly any Bosnian-speaking people in the US. Meeting another Bosnian, randomly, in the streets of New York was very rare. In fact, my friend was the only Bosnian-speaking person I knew. America, especially New York City, was nothing like Sarajevo. It was not the culture I was accustomed to. No one randomly greets you. Everyone seems distant but still respectful. It was not easy fitting in the US or adapt to this culture let alone the language even if it was for only for a three-month vacation. Even though I knew a little English, it was different when you speak with Natives. After three months, I decided to stay here forever because I thought I had a future here-like anyone else I know in the land of opportunity.
>
> A few years later, I got married to an Egyptian man. We lived a very American life style. Neither of us talked about our respective cultures how different or how the same except how we both practiced Islam. We watched American shows and ate American dishes we got used to. We went to Turkish Islamic center.-the only thing we had in common in our cultures. As our girls were growing up, Bosnian or Arabic were not spoken at home. I did not even teach my daughters anything about the culture or even the language. My goal was only to assimilate into the American culture. It was not because I wanted to forget about Bosnian culture but because I wanted to make it easier for my girls. I did not want them to go through what I went through-a cultural shock or cultural confusion.

Figure 5.4. Interfaith Gathering at St Margaret Mary Church in Rochester, NY on Wednesday, August 3, 2016 with women from St. Margaret Mary Church. Fatima Fazlić, (first from the left) during the meeting talked about her journey from Bosnia to Rochester, N.Y.

In 1992, the Bosnian war made everyone interested in the news. I could not believe what was happening to my old childhood country and hometown. I was hurting inside that my birthplace and where I grew up was being destroyed. I thought it was all a dream. I felt guilty like I betrayed my country. I was very surprised that all my life we (Serbians, Croatians, and Bosnians) despite our differences, were all able to live together as one nation and then suddenly we could not. It just seemed so unreal to me.

I was offered a job as an Outreach Advocate, in 1995, when the Bosnian war was over. Bosnian refugees started to settle and, as an Outreach Advocate, I helped them settle in New York City like someone did for me. Even though I am not happy that my country is being torn into pieces. I found a new purpose-to give back to my Bosnian community and to help them assimilate in the same way I once did back in 1978. I was also able to re-live the feelings I once felt when I first came to this country and help alleviate their concerns and problems. Over the years, I started to let the Bosnian culture and language into my daughters' lives because I felt that the Bosnian culture was so rich that it cannot let it be forgotten no matter what. Over time, they started to understand the language and how the Bosnian culture differs from American.

In 1997, I relocated to Rochester, NY and even though I was not offered a position as an Outreach Advocate there as I was in NYC, I still continued to serve as one in this community not only to help them settle in this country but to also interpret English and Bosnian in various situations. I was so amazed that living in the USA the Bosnian culture is still embedded into my life even though I have lived in the US for over 30 years.[190]

---

190. Fatima Fazlić, email to author, January 19, 2017.

HISTORY OF BOSNIAN
ORGANIZATIONS IN ROCHESTER, NY

T he organizing of Bosnian refugees in Rochester started almost immediately after their arrival. At the beginning, it was spontaneous
gatherings, but as time passed, the gatherings became more struc-
tured and in 1995 the first Bosnian Cultural Club was established. Faruk Ferizović, from Banja Luka, Bosnia, who came to Rochester with his mother in
the winter of 1994, was the vice-president of the first Bosnian Culture Club.
In his interview he explained:

> When I first came to Rochester, NY there were about twenty-five
> Bosnian families already in Rochester. They didn't have any formal
> organization but they did get together, especially during holidays.
> When they were not working, Bosnian refugees wanted to get
> together and play soccer and chess. The first soccer club was formed
> in 1995 and was called *Bosnian Culture Club*, located on North
> Clinton. The first president was Ibrahim Grcic and there was a $3
> membership fee for each person. We bought our first team uniforms
> and participated in local soccer tournaments, going around New
> York and Pennsylvania and played against other Bosnian clubs who
> had also already organized themselves.
>
> Unfortunately, this first club existed only for a year and half
> and then people started arguing about alcohol. Some members want-
> ed to bring alcohol to the club and the other members were against
> the idea. A majority of the members stopped paying their member-
> ship and the money was gone, meaning we couldn't afford to pay rent
> or utilities. The club stopped existing, but people still got together at
> their houses, on weddings, and Eid parties.

We organized "Bajramska Sijela" (Eid Parties) in Webster and we had Bosnian music and people felt like they were in Bosnia again, at least for that night. Five years had passed since another club was formed, and it was again the same scenario, until we finally bought our own place and now that is our mosque on 132 Fisher Road in Chili.[191]

Since their first arrival to Rochester, NY, Bosnian refugees mostly used the Turkish mosque located at 853 Culver Rd, Rochester, NY 14609 for their religious needs. Even though the Islamic Center of Rochester sponsored and helped many Bosnian refugees to come to Rochester, the majority of Bosnians felt culturally closer to the Turkish mosque than the Islamic Center of Rochester. This is not surprising, since the Ottomans ruled Bosnia for over four hundred years, and the cultural similarities between these two ethnic groups are immense. Mehmet Aktas, a former Imam at the Turkish Hamidiay Mosque, sponsored and helped many Bosnians refugees settle in Rochester. Imam Mehmet recalls:

Miss Gail, I don't remember her last name, called me from the Catholic Family Center in 1993 and asked me if I would help her sponsor refugees from Bosnia since we share the same faith, Islam. She thought that they would feel more comfortable around Muslims once they arrived in Rochester. I agreed and I sponsored three families and found other Turkish families who also sponsored Bosnian refugees. We met the first group of Bosnian refugees at the Rochester International Airport in 1993. The host families took Bosnian refugees to their homes, and for the next few days we took them from office to office to do the paper work.

The first group of Bosnian refugees did not practice Islamic way of life, did not regularly pray nor they did come to the mosque. However, later on, when other Bosnian refugees arrived, they started asking where they can pray Friday/Jummah Salat, obligatory for males. During Ramadan, they were fasting and coming to the mosque at night, but outside Ramadan, they would come mostly on Friday for the Jummah Salat.

191. Faruk Ferizović, personal interview with author, December 3, 2014.

Bosnians are a hard-working people and they work tirelessly to be financially successful. They are also generous and like to help, but they like to drink alcohol and many do not pray regularly. Even though Bosnian refugees started coming to Rochester in 1993, they still did not start sending their kids in large numbers to the mosque until 1999.[192]

Figure 5.5. Imam Mehmet Aktas, addressing Turkish and Bosnian Community during Eid celebration in 2010 at Turkish Mosque Hamidiye.

Figure 5.6. Bosnian Refugee Children attending Islamic Sunday School at Turkish Hamidiye Mosque , May 2003. From left: Amina Purak, Meliha Kapidzić, Sadmira Hamzic, Zaineb Salem.

192. Imam Mehmed Aktas, personal phone interview with author, August 18, 2016.

Figure 5.7. Bosnian Community in front of Turish Mosque.

On October 26th, 2011, Bosnian refugees finally managed to buy an old church located on 312 Fisher Road, Rochester NY 14624, which they renovated and used as a mosque and for other religious, cultural and social needs. The first and current Imam is Enes Tralješić, who described his journey from Bosnia to Rochester as follows: "My name is Enes Tralješić and I'm 26 years old. Never, in my wildest dreams, could I have imagined that I would ever come to America, let alone that I would live there."[193] He continues his remarks stating how some children dreamed of leaving Bosnia, especially after the war, but he was not one of them since none of his immediate family lived abroad, and only a few members of my extended family lived in other European countries. After finishing primary school and high school, he had the opportunity to study in the capital of Bosnia and Herzegovina.

---

193. Enes Tralješić, email to the author, November 26, 2014.

Figure 5.8. Teacher, Aiša Purak with her students at Turkish and Bosnian Eid celebration in 2010 at Turkish Mosque Hamidiye.

He knew that his chances of success greatly increased with a completed college degree from Sarajevo. That is exactly what happened. After graduation in 2010, he soon received a tourist visa for America. The plan was to stay for six months. However, he realized that there were a lot more opportunities than he had imagined and he continues:

> In Rochester there is a Bosnian Culture Center, which brings together more or less all the Bosniaks of this American city. I got involved in the work of the Center when I first came, fresh from college, and I wanted to help children as much as I could. I volunteered teaching children the Bosnian language, and some of the basics of our religion - Islam. Interestingly, children who were born here have a lot of problems in understanding the Bosnian language, although most of their parents speak Bosnian at home. In a way, you're forced to talk in English because I would definitely be better understood.[194]

Enes further talks about this conversation with the parents who share their experiences and struggles they faced coming to the United States. "I have lived in America for only four years, so I am still getting accustomed to some things, but I get a lot of tips from parents who come to Bosnia & Herzegovina

194. Ibid.

Figure 5.9. Imam Enes Tralješić with her wife Selma during their wedding at the Bosnian Mosque in May, 2013.

Culture Center of Rochester. From conversations with the parents of children, I realized that a new life in the new homeland is not easy."[195]

He continues about how most of our Bosnian immigrants came here after the war, and many of them worked two jobs upon their arrival. In time thank God, that all changed, so that those who worked hard managed to achieve something in their life. A solid number of children are slowly finishing universities and gaining recognitions in various fields, and can spot more beautiful days for the Bosnian people in Rochester. Enough of our people are involved in things you could only dream about in Bosnia, but these dreams managed to be achieved here because they had the most important thing; a chance to show what they know and what they can do. He concludes: "Here in America, if you have the will, you can achieve anything you want because you have the conditions for it. In Bosnia, regardless of the will, effort, talent, or potential, you do not have conditions for some progress or breakthrough. It might happen to some, but it is indeed a rarity."[196]

195. Ibid.
196. Ibid.

REFUGEE RESETTLEMENT PROGRAM CATHOLIC FAMILY CENTER

In the last two decades, the immigration boom has effected Rochester and Monroe County. Even though Rochester did not receive as many Bosnian refugees as some other cities such as Utica, Rochester still has been the adopted home for more the five thousand refugees from former Yugoslavia and the majority of them are from Bosnia and Herzegovina. The refugees from former Yugoslavia started arriving in Rochester in the early 1990s during the Balkan conflict. Catholic Family Center (CFC)[197] and its Refugee, Immigration & Language Services is the only resettlement agency in the Rochester area. CFC Refugee Assistance Programs provided the broad spectrum of services that equipped newly arrived Bosnians with appropriate services, resources, and training.

The Catholic Family Center's Refugee Assistance Program had a very close relationship with local services, ethnic organizations, and faith communities such as the Islamic Center of Rochester and the Turkish Islamic Center. In fact, these two organizations sponsored many Bosnian refugees using the already established and experienced Catholic Family Center. Feda Hadjziosmanovic, Sr. Job Developer at Catholic Family Center and Bosnian refugee himself, said:

> It is hard to estimate the exact number of Bosnian refugees living in Rochester. Unfortunately, the Catholic Family Center did not have a database twenty years ago; therefore we don't know how many Bosnians are living in Rochester at this point. Perhaps in the future, once we scan and organize all of our files, we will have a better idea. But my estimation is that there are around three thousand Bosnians in Rochester and from the former Yugoslavia around two thousand.

---

197. Catholic Family Center (CFC). "History" Source: http://www.cfcrochester.org/about/history/. Retrieved on November 20, 2014.

My estimate is that there are around a total of five thousand descendents from ex-Yugoslavia living in Rochester.[198]

The Catholic Family Center was working with many different groups in Rochester on the resettlement of Bosnian refugees and were very successful. Among these groups were the League of Muslim Women,[199] the Islamic Center of Rochester, the Turkish Islamic Center, and the First Unitarian Church of Rochester, who sponsored and brought many Bosnian refugees. Another Bosnian family who came through League of Muslim Women was the family of Dzaferović; Senada and Jasmin, with their small daughter, Jasmina, who was, at the time, only three years old. Senada's husband Jasmin was in the Omraska Camp.[200] Dževahira Hamzić is another Bosnian who came through League of Muslim Women.

The Catholic Family Center helped Bosnian refugees: find jobs, made their transition at the airport easier, introduced them to the community, assisted them in obtaining social security cards, helped find and furnish homes, and introduced them to services such as English as a Second Language (ESL) training, counseling support, school enrollment for children, connection with public welfare for cash assistance, Food Stamps and health insurance. According to Hadziosmanović, it was easy to work with Bosnians, since they are hard-working people.

I never had an issue finding Bosnians a job. They worked hard and that way they opened doors for more Bosnians to come and work in the same company. In 1993, the Catholic Family Center found jobs for three Bosnians. In 1994 we found jobs for 10 Bosnians. In 1995 we found jobs for 54, in 1996 for 65 Bosnians. In 1997 we found jobs for 170 and the next year for a 198 Bosnians. In 1999 we found jobs for 175 Bosnians and the next year for 116. After that it started decreasing because of the economy. In 2001, we were able to find only 67 jobs and the following year even fewer; we found only 15 jobs and in 2003, only five.[201]

198. Fedja Hadziosmanovic, phone interview with author, November 10, 2014.
199. The League of Muslim Women.Source: http://www.tilmwinc.org/mission-and-vision/. Retrieved on December 5, 2014.
200.The Omarska camp was a death camp run by Bosnian Serb forces in the mining town of Omarska, near Prijedor in northern Bosnia and Herzegovina, set up for Bosniak and Croat men and women during the Prijedor massacre. Retrieved from: http://en.wikipedia.org/wiki/Omarska_camp
201. Hadziosmanovic, telephone interview with author November 10, 2014.

Bosnian Arrivals – Employment Number Between 1993 -2004	
1993	3
1994	10
1995	54
1996	65
1997	170
1998	198
1999	175
2000	116
2001	67
2002	15
2003	5
2004	878

Table. 5.1. Employment Statistics for Bosnian Refugees in Rochester,
N.Y during 1993 – 2004
Source: Refugee Resettlement Services Dept. Catholic Family Center.

CHAPTER SIX

RESEARCH SUMMARY

Bosnians are a hard-working people who take pride in their work and accomplishments. They do not mind working two jobs and saving money in many different ways: preparing food at home, buying vegetables at the public market, going to local farms and picking vegetables and fruits, growing their own vegetables, or buying meat in bulk from local farms. They want to have a house, cars, put children through college and still be able to help families and relatives in Bosnia.

On top of that, they also have a desire to visit their families who still live in Bosnia. A majority of Bosnians had to work two jobs to make any of this possible. It must be noted that in less than a generation, Bosnians in Rochester have become doctors, nurses, teachers, professors, lawyers, insurance agents, bankers, tech specialists, engineers, designers, and entrepreneurs, among others. They bought and remodeled a church and adapted it to a mosque. Quickly they cracked the code of Ameican capitalism and applied it to their own financial successes.

All participants in this survey were Bosnian Muslims who declared that Islam and Bosnian culture play a significant role in their lives. A majority of them were practicing their religion in Bosnia and continued to do so after coming to the United States. However, there were a few participants who did not practice their religion prior to the war. Nevertheless, after their country was attacked and their family members were killed by Serbs or Croats, they started practicing Islam and calling themselves Muslims.

In addition to the group mentioned above, there are a small percent of Bosnian youth who came to America at a very young age and do not even remember their native country Bosnia.

In fact, they do not want to be associated with Bosnians and their culture, religion or language. A few of them agreed to an interview but after questions regarding faith, they subsequently canceled the interview. Most likely, the current media hostility towards Muslims in America is the reason for this uncomfortable behavior. These youth are usually in relationships outside their ethnic group.

Figure 6.1. Bosnian Community in Rochester.

Figure 6.2. Bosnian Community Members renovating their mosque located at 312 Fisher Road in Rochester, NY. BEFORE

Figure 6.3. Bosnian Community Members renovating their mosque located at 312 Fisher Road in Rochester, NY. AFTER

CULTURAL AND RELIGIOUS IDENTITY OF BOSNIAN REFUGEES IN ROCHESTER, NEW YORK

Out of 100 Bosnians who participated in this research, 90% of them said that the Bosnian cuisine is still the only food served on their tables. Working families usually prepare food at night or over the weekend. Bread and sweets are always homemade as Bosnian women take pride in fact that they always make bread and sweets, and that they keep their homes very clean and tidy. Currently there are no ethnic Bosnian stores here in Rochester, but many Bosnians travel to Syracuse or Utica to buy their homeland products. Dishes such as ćevapi, burek and baklava are signature staples of Bosnian cuisine.

Patricia Reed, the American native who was among the first to help Bosnian refugees in Rochester, recalls her first visits to Bosnian homes and eloquently sums up Bosnians' etiquette toward guests:

> When you went to visit someone, they just gave you drinks and food, without asking, and found it extremely rude if you did not drink or eat it all. A huge glass of *sok* (usually soda) filled as close to the very top of the glass as possible, coffee, *keks* and dinner of some sort, a huge chunk of bread, were set in front of you. In the event that you had a second house to visit, it was the same scenario. This was the norm in every household I visited, out came *keks* (which are cookies), and all kind of sweets. After finishing coffee and sweets, if there was to be a meal, it was served after the sweets. This, of course, made no sense to me, but I was beginning to realize that I should not eat too many *keks*! Some people served coffee with sugar cubes, which they dipped into the coffee and then let dissolve in their mouths.

Oh, so many things were strange to me. Pitas, burek, cucumber with tomato salata, chunks of meat cooked outside, homemade bread every day, grah (bean soup), vegeta as a spice, lots of salt and oil for cooking.[202]

Figure 6.4. Typical gathering of Bosnian women in the mosque.

Every single Bosnian family makes baklava and burek for two important holidays; the two Bayrams or Eids, which are the two most important holidays of the Islamic Calendar. One is called Eid-ul-Fitr and is after Ramadan, the other one is called Eid-ul-Adha and comes after Hadz, or the pilgrimage. On both of these holidays, Bosnian families visit each other and share gifts. A majority of them, especially for these two holy days, send money to their relatives in Bosnia and Herzegovina. Usually Eid presents are given to children who are attending Sunday school. On the first Saturday night following Eid, there is a big party to celebrate this event.

During the celebration of these two holidays, the Bosnian community is split into two groups: one group celebrates without serving any alcohol and usually has some religious components incorporated into the program, with traditional food as part of the event, while the other group celebrates the event with alcohol and singers from Bosnia. Below are images taken from various Bosnian gatherings.

202. Reed, ibid.

Figure 6.5.Typical gathering of Bosnian community in the mosque.

Figure 6.6. Traditional Bosnian Dance kolo 2010.

Figure 6.7. Choir Sabur.

Figure 6.8. Bosnian refugees from Rochester hosting lunch for Bosnian refugees from Syracuse and Utica on Sunday, March 20, 2011 at 1039 North Greece Road.

RESEARCH SUMMARY

D espite the large number of Bosnians in Rochester, roughly about three thousand, only 150 families are paid members of the Bosnian mosque. A vast majority of Bosnians do not come to the mosque, nor do they take any interest in its organization. The community is sharply divided. One group is more empathic to the cultural part of Bosnian tradition, including music and dance. This group promotes parties with Bosnian traditional songs and dancing, where youth can meet and get to know each other, which eventually will lead towards more marriages among Bosnians.

The other group is more for religious organization and events. They want to have an Imam who will be a magnet to attract and connect Bosnians as well as to lead the prayers and teach their children about Islam using the Bosnian language. This group wants to have many events but with religious content and fewer cultural component. This group would love to see at least all five daily prayers offered during the weekend, Jummah salat, Iftars, breaking of fast during Ramadan, and all religious holidays celebrated in this mosque. Also, this group pushes for more programs for women, children, and youth. For this group, it is imperative to have a Bosnian Imam who will teach the community Islamic values and teach the younger generation in the Bosnian language.

This will ensure that the Bosnian language is preserved and with time and constant preaching, alcohol consumption and divorce rates will decrease. Both groups, however, agree that they should have a mosque and an Imam. The mosque should have Islamic Studies and Qur'an classes, but they disagree in which language this should be taught. The first group argues that English is a better language for youth since they understand it better and

Figure 6.9. Choir Sabur performing at the Memorial Art Gallery.

Imam does not necessarily have to be Bosnian. The Bosnian language should be taught and spoken at home.

The second group argues that everything must be taught in Bosnian so that the younger generation will learn and keep their language. Both groups also agree upon having many different youth sections or activities, such as Bosnian traditional dancing or singing, soccer or tennis team. Many attempts have been made to organize youth throughout different activities. Many have been very successful; for instance, the dance group *Sevdah* or choir *Sabur* have been performing at many Bosnian or Turkish events. Both of these groups have been invited to perform at other Bosnian annual festivals across the United States as well as International festivals at Brockport and Memorial Art Gallery.

A Bosnian soccer team also made noticeable success playing against other Bosnian clubs in Upstate New York, as well as other ethnic groups in the Greater Rochester area. Emma Strujo, a twenty year old Bosnian, born in Rochester, New York, writes about her views on Bosnia.

Figure 6.10. Bosnian Folk Dancing group in 2006.

Figure 6.11. Damir Husamović holding trophy from soccer tournament in
Syracuse on May 28, 2009.

I am a proud daughter of Bosnian refugees. My parents and brother came to the United States of America in 1995. I was born shortly after in 1996 in Rochester, NY. My parents have always called me their "Welcome to America gift". To me, being a Bosnian girl means more than words can ever describe. I am beyond blessed to have the family I do and my heritage because I think Bosnia I Herzegovina is a very sacred and cherished place. It is my favorite place and I have visited ever since I was 3 years old. Every time I go back to visit I feel like I was born there and never left because of the sense of unity that fills my heart when I see my family and friends.

Figure 6.12. Emma Strujo with her family.

My parents taught me the Bosnian language before I learned any English and from then on I have always had an enormous connection to my culture. Before 9/11 I never felt different from any other kids in school or around my community. After the tragic attack in the U.S. my Bosnian friends and I experienced hateful comments toward us for being Muslim. However, no amount of bullying has ever made me regret being Muslim. I have always been honored and grateful to tell people where I come from and who I am.

Even though I am not religious I know that Islam is a religion of peace. People look at the Islamic religion when there are terrorist attacks because the radical Islamists use Islam for their attacks and kill innocent people including innocent Muslims. This is something that has bothered me for a long time because people always assume that all Muslims are bad when they have yet to meet kind and generous Muslim families. I hope one day more people will learn about the Islam religion and how it brings people together to love and not hate. I have had the fortune of being born into a Bosnian family who have always supported me, loved me, worked hard, and given me a wonderful life.[203]

Zaineb Salem, a second generation Bosnian-American, has a Bosnian mother and an Arab father. Initially, her mother came to New York City in 1974 to learn English. She lived in New York City and eventually moved to Rochester with her two daughters and sister. Here is how Zaineb Salem, a thirty-two years old woman, sees Bosnia and Bosnian Community:

I was born into a multi-cultural family. My mother was born in Sarajevo, Bosnia and my father was born in Alexandria, Egypt. But I was born in Brooklyn, New York, USA. Despite the very different cultural backgrounds, in our household, we emerged mostly into the American culture upbringing. We all spoke English in the house, despite my parents' abilities to speak their corresponding mother tongue with us or around us. We also watched American shows and ate American-style foods.

203. Emma Stujo, email to the author, January 25, 2017.

The only thing that we were taught differently at home was to practice Islam and celebrate different holidays other than what was taught in school. Occasionally, we would visit our parents friends separately. My mother would take us to her Bosnian- speaking friends or go to the Bosnian Society Mosque. Likewise, my father would take us to visit his Arabic- speaking friends and go to the Islamic Center as well. Even though neither parent took the time to teach us, actively, their mother tongue, I developed the ability to understand the Bosnian language just from hearing my mother speak to her friends and long distance family. The only one thing that was in common was that Family values were very well stressed. The ability to pick up the Bosnian language was not a skill I could do with Arabic as a child. I was able to also see the differences in cultures among the three and how are they all alike. The only one thing that was in common was that Family values were very well stressed.

In 1995, everything completely changed and so did my Bosnian knowledge and skills. There was influx of Bosnian refugees settling into New York City. My mother went from being a stay-at- home mom to working as an Outreach Advocate for the Bosnian Community. People used to call our house after working hours asking to speak with my mother and I knew that they could not speak English. I found myself wanting to respond back but could not immediately. I had a barrier that I must overcome. The Influx of Bosnian refugees motivated me to start trying harder in speaking Bosnian more than just understanding words. Each time people called, I responded the way my mother used to greet them. After school, my mother would take me to the office and I would listen to them discussing their concerns in Bosnian.

I began to try to imitate the way they spoke to each other including adapting to their demeanor and their idioms. In less than a year, I started to speak in complete sentences with a fewer grammatical mistakes which the English language knows nothing about.

As I got older, we re-located to Rochester, NY where the Bosnian Community was even stronger. Everyone knew each other and communicated on a daily basis. My Bosnian knowledge became stronger because you could not go a day without speaking in Bosnian where ever you went. In fact, they used to call Rochester, "little Bosnia" and eventually, the Bosnian Cultural Center was created. Even studying abroad or leaving Rochester for a few months to years, "little Bosnia" was still home to me. It was a place where we can forget anything and relax with good friends we considered as our extended family.

In 2012, I was lucky enough to go Sarajevo, Bosnia for about a month where I was able to see a different side of the Bosnian culture-where it all began. I realized the Bosnian culture both in the USA and in Bosnia were nearly identical- their practices, beliefs and way of life was nearly the same. Even being there for just three days in *Čarsija*, you could not avoid the locals without starting to greet you as one of their own just like in "Little Bosnia, Rochester." What appealed to me about going to see my mother's birthplace was not only to compare and contract cultures but also to relive my mother's life before I was born. I started to share the special things she, once, cherished. We developed as stronger bond not only as mother and daughter but as "Sarajke."[204]

204. Zaineb Salem, personal interview and email to the author, January 15, 2017.

SURVEY RESULTS

O ut of 35 Bosnian household participants in the survey, 13 were female and 22 were male. The age varied from 18 to 78 years old. One of the participantso was between 18-29 years, 22 participants were between the ages of 30-49, 10 participants were between the ages 50-64 and 2 participants were 65 or older. Out of the 35 participants: 27 were married, 2 were never married, 5 were divorced and 1 participant declined to answer. Many Bosnian refugees divorced after they came to this new culture. Women are more prone to initiate divorce here in America than in Bosnia.

The primary reason was their new-found economic independence, which gives many females opportunities they never had before. The new society also had a kinder attitude towards divorce than the old one. Almost all of these women divorcees who participated in this survey initiated the divorce, after their children were already grown up and their parents had passed away. They had issues in their marriages prior to coming to America, but they had no opportunity to take care of themselves or their children, hence their delayed decision to obtain a divorce. In Bosnia, tradition dictates that divorce is a very shameful act and must be avoided. The community pressure and shame is still present among Bosnians in Rochester.

Out of the majority of Bosnians (25 out 35) who arrived here in the United States between 1990 and 2000, 8 arrived between 2001-2014 and one participant was born here in the United States. The Bosnian refugees who came to Rochester are from all occupations. They came from different regions of Bosnia, as well as representing various socio-economic and education levels.

When they first arrived in Rochester, these differences did not matter. However, with time, people started to group according their regional up-bringings in Bosnia. According to Senada Dzaferović, who was among the first to arrive in Rochester: "The connection and understanding among Bosnian families at the beginning was very good. We supported each other, helped each other, and visited each other. At the beginning, there were about forty families and we all were like one family. Unfortunately, with time, things changed. Now we barely see each other. We simply grew apart. I miss those times, but I guess we got busy with our kids and grandchildren."[205]

Figure 6.13. Senada Dzaferovic with her daughter Jasmina.

205. Senada Dzaferovic, telephone interview with author, Dec 07, 2014.

As far as education, of the thirty-five participants who took the survey, fourteen of them have a high school degree or less, two have some college, nine of them have an Associate's degree and nine have a Bachelor's degree. One participant has their Master's Degree. None of the participants has a PhD or Doctoral degree or any professional degree. Out of thirty-five participants, eight have no children, six have one child, fourteen have two children, six have three children and one family has four children.

SURVEY GENERAL TRENDS IN MUSLIM BOSNIAN COMMUNITY IN ROCHESTER, NY					
Income		Education		Family Status	
less than $25,000	5	High School or Less	14	Married	27
$25,000 - $50,000	11	Some College	2	Divorced	5
$50,000 - $75,000	7	Associate Degree	9	Single	1
$75,000 - $100,000	7	Bachelor's Degree	9	Widow/Widower	1
$100,000- $125,000	3	Masters	1	Didn't Answer	1
$125,001- $150,000	0	Professional Degree	0	Total	35
More than $150,000	1	PhD or Doctorate	0		
Didn't Answer	1	Didn't Answer	0		
Total	35	Total	35		

Table 6.1 Survey[206] is based on 35 Bosnian Muslim community of Greater Rochester area, NY

Out of the thirty-five survey participants, twenty-seven are homeowners and eight are renters. The Real Estate of all participants is valued between $60,000 to $400,000. The majority of Bosnian refugees live in Greece, Charlotte, Irondequoit, Webster and Henrietta. Lately, a good number of Bosnians have been purchasing homes in Penfield and Fairport.

206. The purpose of this survey was to obtain a general trend in the Bosnian Muslim community of Greater Rochester area. The purpose of the survey was to obtain only a general data. Collected data will be also used in a monographic publication titled: History of the Islamic Center of Rochester and Muslim Ethnic Communities of Rochester. The book will only mention trends in the Muslim community. No personal Information will be published. The survey for the Bosnian community was conducted in 2004 and 2015.

The majority of participants who took the survey have either completely paid off their home mortgages or are very close to doing so. Some of them are building and moving to a second house, like Emira Mujičić, who is a real estate agent: "My family got bigger. Now I have three kids, my in-laws, my husband and I. We are a family of seven people and my current house is getting small for us. My kids are getting bigger and everyone wants to have more privacy. Moving to our new bigger house is convenient and the best solution for everybody. Best of all, I'll be closer to my parents' house."[207]

Businesses here in Rochester started by Bosnian immigrants include real estate, construction companies, restaurants, cleaning companies, car dealerships, computer programming businesses, truck operators, and hair stylists. Out of the thirty-five participants, nine of them own their business, while twenty-six of them work for other companies. Two of them operate restaurants, one has a cleaning company, two have real estate businesses and four have car dealerships. Overall, more Bosnians are trying their luck in running their own business. Some of them are forced to open their business because of health issues or war wounds, like Zijad Hamzić.

Figure 6.14. Zijad Hamzić with his wife Zineta and their three daughters and son in law during his daughter's wedding, September 2013.

207. Emira Mujicic, phone interview with author, December 10, 2014.

Zijad Hamzić is a Bosnian refugee who was wounded in the Bosnian war and came to Rochester in hopes of saving his leg, which was seriously damaged in the war. After arriving in Rochester with his wife and two daughters, he started to learn English, and soon began attending Monroe Community College. Soon afterwards, along with his wife, he started working for a company, and stayed there as an employee for five years. After five years, the company went out of business, and Zijad decided to try his luck with opening his own car dealership.

> All those years, while I was working in the company, I experienced chronic severe pains in my leg. It was almost unbearable for me to stand on my wounded leg for more than eight or ten hours every day, but I had to because of my two daughters and family. I didn't want my daughters to suffer, and not to have things like other kids because of my wounded leg. I was determined to work and provide all that I could, so they could have a normal childhood here in America. Unfortunately, I did not get much help for my leg recovery here. There were some complications with the papers and I guess the treatment was just too expensive.
>
> Meanwhile, I decided to open my own business because I was not able to stand for a long time and I thought once I have my own business, I could choose my hours and my work according to my personal needs, and so far it has been working out well. I have been in the car dealership business for well over ten years now and this works best for me. Even though most of the time, I still work more hours than I would like, it is still better for me because I can take a break or sit if the leg pain becomes too severe. I am very thankful to God that I am still able to provide for my family.[208]

Many Bosnian refugees, like other immigrants around the world, came to the United States hoping to find a myriad of easy money. However, in America, like everywhere else in the world, money does not grow on trees. What they did find, however, was the opportunity to work and provide for their families; which is still lacking in Bosnia.

---

208. Zijad Hamzic, telephone interview with author, December 03, 2014.

Figure 6.15. Midhat Purak with his daughter Amina in 2015.

Midhat Purak, a truck driver, said, "If I didn't get into the trucking business I would go back to Bosnia. I tried everything: restaurant business, contracting business, manufacturing business and nothing worked for me. Since I am in the trucking business, I am very happy. I get to see America; there is almost no state I have not visited. America is a beautiful land, and I am glad that I traveled and experienced this unique and powerful country."[209]

Out of 35 participants in this survey, 28 are registered and vote. The majority, 32 out of 35, are affiliated with the Democratic Party, one is affiliated with the Republican Party, and one with the Independent Party. One participant declined to answer this question. On the survey question asking about Bosnian community organization involvement, 15 out of 35 answered that they were involved, while 20 answered that they were not. On the question regarding community voting, 18 out of 35 answered that they vote, while 16 answered that they did not. One participant did not answer.

209. Midhat Purak, personal interview with author, October 15, 2014.

Survey		
General Trends in Muslim Bosnian Community in Rochester, NY		

Time of Arrival to USA		How Many Children		What is your political affiliation?	
Between 1960 and 1970	0	None	8	Republican	0
Between 1971 and 1981	0	One	5	Democrat	34
Between 1981 and 1990	0	Two	12	Independent	0
Between 1990 and 2000	25	Three	8	DID NOT ANSWER	1
Between 2001 and 2014	8	Four or More	2	Total	35
I was born in the USA	2	Didn't Answer	0		
Didn't Answer	0	Total	35		
Total	30				

Table 6.2. Survey General Trends in Muslim Bosnian Community in Rochester, NY.

CONCLUSION

Over three thousand Bosnian Muslims have made Rochester, NY their home after being forced to flee their country in the early 1990s, losing everything, and having to endure the pain of losing family members and friends. Through hard work and dedication, they proved themselves a good addition to this city. However, there are very serious challenges that lie ahead of the Bosnian community in Rochester. Further research is needed to thoroughly explore and evaluate the historic development and current situation of the Bosniaks' immigration into the United States and Rochester.

It can be concluded that the Bosnian community in Rochester, even from the early days was connected, in one way or another. Even after more than twenty years living in Rochester, Bosnians remain connected. Firstly, they remain connected through a variety of personally organized gatherings: sijela, birthday parties, weddings, bridal and baby shower, holidays and verias religious gathering. Secondly, they organized themselves through sports and cultural clubs.

Lastly, they organized themselves through religious connections, creating an organization that still exists. The formal name of the Bosnian mosque is Bosnia & Herzegovina Culture Center of Rochester (BHCC) and is located on 312 Fisher Rd., Rochester, NY 14624. Below is a chronological list of some Bosnian organizations and activities in Rochester, NY. However, it must be noted that all these dates listed below are based on information provided by Bosnians during our interviews and in most cases, there are not official documents available.

Figure 6.16. First community event in a new building in 2010. Photo shows program participants during this event.

1993: The first group of Bosniaks came from Bosnia and Herzegovina
in Rochester, NY.

1995: Establishment of the first Bosnian Soccer Club called *Bosnian
Cultural Club*.

1999: First year of religious classes for Bosnian kids in the Turkish
Hamidiye Mosque.[210]

2000: First year of a summer camp for Bosnian kids in the Turkish
Hamidiye Mosque.

2000: First Women Religions gatherings. First lectures, mevlud and
socializing for Muslim women in the Turkish mosque *Hamidiye*.

2001: First attempt at organizing the Bosniak Jama'at Rochester.

2002: Launch of the Bosnian Soccer Club.

2002: Foundation of the *KUD Sevdah* (Bosnian Folk Dance Group).

2008: Start of teaching Bosnian language and religion on Lake Ave.

2009: Establishment of Sunday school for Bosnian children in

Turkish *Hamidiye* mosque and Formal establishment of choir *Sabur*.

---

210. Islamic Culture Center - Rochester, NY & Hamidiye Mosque is official name but, Bosnian community adapted *Turkish Mosque* name and it was widely used among Bosnians.

2009: Bosnian community in Rochester officially joins the Islamic Community Of North American Bosniaks (ICNAB).[211]
2009: Religion classes for kids begin at the Turkish Culture Center at North Greece.
2010: Employment of first Bosnian Imam in Rochester
2010: First Religious gathering in a new building.
2011: Purchase and full payment of the church at Fisher Road – current Bosnian Mosque.
2011: First Bosnian food festival in Rochester.

The Bosnia and Herzegovina Cultural Center hosts meetings and events for the Bosnian Community of both cultural and religious significance. Many events are hosted there, including weddings, birthday parties, religious events, sporting activities, humanitarian events etc. Even though many Bosnians are not paying members, all are welcome to use this facility.

Nevertheless, it must be noticed that after only twenty years of living in Rochester, NY, a majority of Bosnians are already living the American dream. After losing and leaving everything they had in Bosnia, they strived for a better life through hard work and the endless opportunities this country offered. A majority of them live in their-almost paid off-houses, own at least one car, have at least one child who has earned a college degree, all while still managing to financially support families and relatives in Bosnia.

It can be therefore concluded that Bosnian immigrants in America, specifically Rochester, can only prosper and keep their identity intact if they shield their family with religious and culturally tight organizations, keep strong and firm connections with Bosnia, but avoid complete segregation from the new culture. Otherwise, they will continuously experience early pregnancy and running away cases that already affect the Rochester Bosnian community. Dozens of young girls and boys alike are running away from their strict and traditional Bosnian families.

211. ICANB: Islamic Community of Norht American Bosniaks. "ICNAB is the premiere umbrella organization representing the cross-section of over 200,000 Bosniak Muslims in the U.S. and Canada. By way of its membership, ICNAB has the knowledge, contacts and long-standing relationships to both reach out to and represent this scattered Muslim American community." Source: http://icnab.com/index.php/english/about-icnab. Retrieved on January 25,2017.

Drug abuse, primarily alcohol abuse, is heavily present in Bosnian homes. Many Bosnian men drink heavily on the weekends, while barely maintaining sobriety during the weekdays. While high school dropouts are not a widespread phenomenon in the Bosnian community, there are a few instances. Divorce rates in the Bosnian community are on the rise. While economic and educational prosperity is clearly improving within the Bosnian community, the challenges mentioned above are clouding this progress, and the gap between generations is widening. This work suggests that the first Bosnian generations must be a bridge between the two worlds so their children can safely move from one world to another and not to feel trapped in either of them.

As stated, the purpose of this research was to research socially the first Bosnian immigrants who came to the United States of America. In particularly Rochester, and to analyze and understand the experiences of these Bosnian families in regards to their lives prior to the war, their experiences during the war, and the lives they lead here in Rochester. More than twenty years have passed since the first Bosnian refugees integrated as Rochestarians. After twenty years of living in this new society, it could be said with some degree of certainty that it was inevitable for Bosnians to be so culturally, politically and economically shaped and influenced by the host societies.

Their religious and cultural identity was suppressed by the communist philosophy, which considers religion as a moral weakness, and being a practicing Muslim was regarded as shameful. This upbringing had a tremendous effect on the culture of Bosnian Muslims who currently live in Rochester. Therefore, many Bosnian Muslims are still not part of the Bosnian religious organization called Jema'at, and have issues with their religious and cultural identity. This insecurity about their own religious and cultural identity is encoded in them from Bosnia. Even though, further research is needed on this issue, in her written interview Merjema Purak, who came to America when she was three years old, perfectly summed up the identity crises among Bosnian youth living in Rochester, NY.

Figure 6.17. Merjema Purak during her high school graduation in 2014.

Although I hadn't been born yet, the Bosnian War has affected me in more ways than can ever be transcribed, because so much of my identity stems from my Bosnian roots. Although I was three when we moved to America, I have always thought of myself as Bosnian, even though I haven't always been so confident in my heritage. For as long as I can remember, I have been told I was Bosnian. Sure, I spoke the language, practiced the religion, even did a presentation on it for the 3rd grade Heritage Fair, but what did it mean to be part of a nation? For my parents' home to be different than my own? I had only ever known America, and while we were far from the typical American family, we also weren't quite the standard Bosnian household. It wasn't until I was 9 and went on my first trip to the country that I began to understand quite how integral the far off land was in my life, and how it helped define who I am.

Before anything gets better, it gets worse. I had hoped that by visiting my homeland, I would get a better sense of who I was, or where I belong, but I simply felt more lost. I was constantly surrounded by strangers, hugging me, asking me questions, commenting on how much I've grown. Even as I grew more comfortable, it wasn't what I was hoping for. Somewhere, at some point in my life, I had gotten the idea that Bosnia was a fairytale land where I would be completely like all the other kids, and my family would completely fit in, but that was far from true.

My extended family is mostly comprised of farmers, and farming was how most of my time passed. It was unlike anything I had experienced before, and it was obvious by my farming ineptitude. Everyone fixated on the differences between us. How different America was, how I had never done farm work, how my clothes were different, how my Bosnian wasn't flawless. Here, in this land of my people, I was more isolated than in America. Now, I don't mean to imply I felt alone in America. On the contrary, I had many friends, from school, tennis, the mosque, and simply old family-Bosnian-friends.

I was never bullied or mocked, but I never found someone exactly like me, and that was what I was searching, even yearning for. And I had created a version of Bosnia where I was surrounded by people all like me, and I would have the greatest time. I may not have found a second Merjema, but I did have a wonderful time. I came to understand that there is not a single other living human being who is just like me. As cliched as that may sound, I realized I am one of a kind. No one else would have the exact same thoughts, experiences, or memories. While this may seem obvious to some, it was a great struggle to overcome for someone fighting between two drastically different worlds. Why would I pick one, when I could be part of both? This has been, and will continue to be, my personal motto, as I continue living as a Bosnian American.[212]

Perhaps the best way to finish this research paper is with a statement from Bosnian Historian, Murat Mahmutović. In his book, *Krvavi Praznici –genocid nad Bošnjacima (Bloody Holidays -genocides against Bosniaks)*, he argues that if a nation wants to be morally, ethnically and religiously awakened, its inhabitants should know their history, as it is, without distortion of facts through politicization or manipulation. Bosniaks have gone through a century of struggle: their right to vote was always taken away from them. Today, after much agonizing for the Bosniaks, a good portion of the population is still not familiar with the suffering of their ancestors, relatives and family. This is certainly a result of manipulated historical writings in which oppressors are presented as heroes and defenders of honor. The history of Bosniaks has always been written by their oppressors. He concludes that now is the time for Bosnian people to write about their history and to tell their story from their perspective.[213]

This work is an addition to the growing trend of Bosnians recording their own history. This work is a pioneering study on the history of Bosnia and Bosnian refugees in Rochester, NY. It should be an important read both by military and socio-political historians to study the background of modern Yugoslavia.

---

212. Merjema Purak, email sent to author, December 2016.
213. Murat Mahmutovic, *Krvavi praznici genocidi nad Bošnjacima* (Novi Pazar: El-Kelimeh, 2014).

Additionally, it is a significant addition to the study of Serbian-Bosnian relations, as well as the study of the Muslim minority in the former Yugoslavia.
This paper also analyses how, after the split from Yugoslavia, Serbs tried
to control and dominate Bosniaks and take away their Muslim identity. It
clearly amplifies the failures of interfaith relations among Greek Orthodox,
Catholics, and Muslims, even though a good number of Bosnians Muslims
were married to Serbs and Croats. Many Bosnian Refugees who were in
interfaith marriages ended up in Rochester.

This book specifically tackles pressing issues including trauma, alcohol
abuse and the increasing divorce rate, as well as the ever-growing division
inside the Bosnian community. Further research on the Bosnian community in Rochester is highly recommended, specifically addressing challenges
that the Bosnian community is facing, focusing on divisions and differences
between generations. Youth should be a focal point because of the prevalent identity crises and marital challenges, while older Bosnians experience
nostagia, loneliness, and a lack of dependence. Relations between the generations are also vital because older generations preserve the traditions they
wish to pass on to the younger Bosnian Americans.

According to the Bosnian Americans with whom I interviewed, their
deepest desire for their children is a chance to further their education, to earn
diplomas that will eventually provide them with a more prosperous future.
Bosnian Americans take pride in their children's education, often bragging
to their relatives in Bosnia. It elevates them to a higher social status within
their own community and in society as a whole. Despite their own economic
well being, education take precedence. They see their children's education as
their own success. They consider formal education as job security for their
children and the key to success here in the United States.

Furthermore, this research enriches American diversity and will be ben-
eficial for new refugees forced to emigrate from their home. It is important
because we can learn from the experiences of Bosnian Refugees both coming
to the United States and during the war in Bosnia, where they were victims
of genocide.

APPENDIX

SURVEY
September 5, 2014

In 1967 The Muslim community in Rochester was only about 25 people, but today it is about 25 thousand. Currently, they are twelve Mosques in the Greater Rochester area. The purpose of this survey is to obtain a general trend in the Muslim community of Greater Rochester area. We want to obtain only a general data. Collected data will be used in a monographic publication titled: *History of the Islamic Center of Rochester and Muslim Ethnic Communities of Rochester*. The book will only mention trends in the Muslim community. No personal information will be published. If there is any question you don't want to answer, you can skip it and go on to the next one. It is not essential to answer all questions in this survey, especially, those that you don't feel comfortable answering.

Please check the box that is applicable to you

1. WHAT IS YOUR GENDER?

   ☐ Male

   ☐ Female

2. WHAT IS YOUR AGE?

   ☐ 18-29

   ☐ 30-49

   ☐ 50-64

   ☐ 65 and Older

3. COUNTRY OF ORIGIN?

   ☐ _____

4. LIST NATIVE AND OTHER LANGUAGES YOU SPEAK

   ☐ _____

   ☐ _____

5. WHEN DID YOU COME TO THE USA?

   ☐ Between 1960 and 1970

   ☐ Between 1971-1980

   ☐ Between 1981 – 1990

   ☐ Between 1990 – 2000

   ☐ Between 2001 – 2014

   ☐ I was born in the USA

6. WHAT IS THE HIGHEST DEGREE YOU HAVE ATTAINED?

   ☐ High School or Less

   ☐ Some College

   ☐ Associate degree

   ☐ Bachelor's degree

   ☐ Masters

   ☐ Professional degree

   ☐ PhD or doctorate

7. ANNUAL FAMILY INCOME

   ☐ Less than $25,000

   ☐ $25,001-$50,000

   ☐ $50,001 - $75,000

   ☐ $75,001-$100,000

   ☐ $100,001-$125,000

   ☐ $125,001-$150,000

   ☐ More than $150,000

8. MARITAL STATUS

   ☐ Married

   ☐ Single

   ☐ Divorced

   ☐ Widow/widower

9. HOW MANY CHILDREN DO YOU HAVE

SURVEY

September 5, 2014

☐ None

☐ One

☐ Two

☐ Three

☐ Four or more

10. HOW MANY CHILDREN ARE ATTENDING
    COLLEGE

☐ One

☐ Two

☐ Three

☐ Four or more

☐ Not applicable

11. HOW MANY CHILDREN FINISHED COLLEGE

☐ One

☐ Two

☐ Three

☐ Four or more

☐ Not applicable

12. HOW MANY ARE PURSUING PROFESSIONAL
    DEGREE/S

☐ One

☐ Two

☐ Three

☐ Four or more

☐ Not applicable

13. HOW MANY HAVE FINISHED
    PROFESSIONAL DEGREE/S , PLEASE
    INDICATE THE DEGREE

☐ One

☐ Two

☐ Three

☐ Four or more

☐ _____

☐ _____

14. WHAT IS THE PRIMARY LANGUAGE/S
    SPOKEN IN YOUR HOUSEHOLD?

☐ English

☐ Arabic

☐ Urdu

☐ Bosnian

☐ Turkish

☐ Other (specify)_____

15. ARE YOU A HOME OWNER?

☐ Yes

☐ No

16. DO YOU OWN A BUSINESS?

☐ Yes

☐ no (skip question 15)

17. IF YES, HOW MANY PEOPLE DO YOU
    EMPLOY?

☐ 0 – 5

☐ 6 – 10

☐ 11 – 15

☐ 16 – 20

☐ More than 20

18. DO YOU VOTE?

☐ Yes

☐ No

19. WHAT IS YOUR POLITICAL AFFILIATION?
    (PLEASE CHECK ONE)

☐ Republican

☐ Democrat

☐ Independent

20. HAVE YOU EVER PARTICIPATED IN A POLITICAL CAMPAIGN? (PLEASE CHECK ONE)

☐ YES

☐ NO

21. HAVE YOU EVER MADE A POLITICAL DONATION? (PLEASE CHECK ONE)

☐ YES

☐ NO

22. HAVE YOU EVER ORGANIZED A FUNDRAISER FOR A CANDIDATE (PLEASE CHECK ONE)

☐ NO

☐ YES

☐

23. ARE YOU INVOLVED IN YOUR COMMUNITY ORGANIZATION?

☐ YES

☐ NO

24. ARE YOU INVOLVED IN YOUR COMMUNITY VOTING?

☐ YES

☐ NO

25. WHEN DID YOU JOIN THE ICR

☐ Between 1960 and 1970

☐ Between 1971-1980

☐ Between 1981 – 1990

☐ Between 1990 – 2000

☐ Between 2001 – 2014

26. HAVE YOU HELD ANY OFFICE IN PASOR?

☐ Yes

☐ No

27. HOW DO YOU RATE ISLAMIC CENTER OF ROCHESTER?

☐ Excellent
☐ Very Good
☐ Good
☐ Average
☐ Poor

28. DOES YOUR MOSQUE MEET ALL COMMUNITY NEEDS?

☐ Yes
☐ No
☐ Some
☐ Other (Specify) _____

_____

PLEASE FEEL FREE TO ADD ANY PERSONAL EXPERIENCES, REMARKS OR COMMENTS ON THE ISLAMIC CENTER THEY WILL BE GREATLY APPRECIATED.

_____

_____

For extra space please use the back of the page

BIBLIOGRAPHY:

PRIMARY SOURCE:

Aktas, Mehmed. Personal phone interview with author, August 18, 2016.

Anonymous. E-mail message to author, November 26, 2014.

Bečirović, Mediha. Personal interview with author, December 3, 2014.

Bibić, Minka. Personal interview with author, November 11, 2014.

Bodulović, Amela. E-mail message to author, November 27, 2014.

Džaferović, Senada.Telephone interview with author, Dec 07, 2014.

Fazlić, Sidreta. Personal interview with author, on August 22, 2016.

Fazlić, Kadrija. Personal interview with author, September 1, 2016.

Ferizović-Dolić , Faruk. Personal interview with author, August 14, 2015.

Gobeljić, Hasiba. Conversation with author, July 2016 at the Bosnia Cultural Center.

Hadžiosmanović, Feda. Catholic Family Center Senior Job Developer, telephone interview, November 15, 2014.

Hadžić, Remza. Personal interview with author, December 26, 2016.

Hamzić, Dževahira. Personal interview with author, September 1, 2016.

Hamzić, Zijad. Telephone interview with author, December 03, 2014.

Jusić, Ismeta. Personal interview with author, August 23, 2015.

Kapić, Refija. Personal interview with author, September 1, 2016.

Kapić, Muharem. Personal interview with author, September 1, 2016.

Kapidžić, Meho. Telephone interview with author, January 15, 2015.

Kolobodanović, Sadika. Personal interview with author, August 14, 2015.

Kurspahić, Eniz. Personal interview with author, September 1, 2016.

Malik, Salahuddin. Personal interview with author, October 25, 2015.

Mutapčić, Denisa. Personal interview with author, November 11, 2014.

Nadž, Frank. Telephone interview with author, December 03, 2014.

Pehlivanović, Senada. Personal interview with author, August 14, 2015.

Purak, Merjema Personal interview with author, October 15, 2014.

Purak, Midhat. Personal interview with author, October 15, 2014.

Rastoder, Zejto. Personal interview with author, August 18, 2015.

Razić, Fatima. Personal interview with author via Facebook, December 22, 2016.

Reed, Patricia. Personal communication, October, 2014.

R.O. Personal interview with the author, August 2014.

Salem, Zaineb. Personal interview and email to the author, January 15, 2017.

Spahić, Amel e-mail message to author, November 20, 2014.

Salkanović, Fatima. Facebook message to author, October 10, 2016.

Stenaklić, Halima. Personal interview with author, November 11, 2014.

Strujo, Emma. Email message to author, January 25, 2017.

Tralješić, Enes. Email to author, November 26, 2014.

SECONDARY SOURCE:

Agić, Senad. *Immigration and Assimilation: The Bosnian Muslim Experience in Chicago.* (Lima, Ohio: Wyndham Hall Press, 2004).

Agić, Senad. *100 godina Bosnjaka u Americi = A Centennail of Bosniaks in America*: (Chicago: Bosnian American Cultural Association; Islamic Association of Bosniaks in North America, 2006).

Al-Ahari, Muhammed. *A Heritage of East and West: The Writings of Imam Camil Avdić.* (Chicago: Magribine Press, 2006).

Allen, Beverly. *Rape warfare: The hidden genocide in Bosnia- Herzegovina and Croatia*. (Minneapolis: University of Minnesota Press. 1996).

Avdich, Kamil. *Survey of Islamic Doctrine*. (Cedar Rapids, Iowa: Unity, 1979).

Bloemraad, Irene. *Becoming a citizen: Incorporating immigrants and refugees in the United States and Canada*. (Berkeley: University of California Press. 2006).

Cigar, Norman. *Genocide in Bosnia: The Policy of Ethnic Cleansing*. (TX: Texas A and M University Press, 2000).

Čelebi, Evlija. *Putopis: odlomci o jugoslavenskim zemljama*. (Sarajevo: Svjetlost, 1967).

Davis ,G. Scott. *Religion and Justice in the War over Bosnia*. (New York: Routledge 1996).

Donia ,Robert and VA Fine, John. *Bosnia and Hercegovina: A Tradition Betrayed*. (Columbia University Press. 2005), pg.73. Retrieved 30 October 2012.

Enver, Imamović. *Da li je rimska Arduba današnji Vranduk u Bosni*. (Sarajevo: Prilozi Instituta za istoriju XIV. 14-151978), 337 – 347.

Hazen, Julianne. "Contemporary Islamic Sufism in America: The Philosophy and Practices of the Alami Tariqa in Waterport" (New York. PhD Work, SOAS, University of London, 2011).Source: http://eprints.soas.ac.uk/13816/1/Hazen_3369.pdf.

Lovrenović, Ivan. *Bosnia: A Cultural History*. (New York: New York University Press. 2001).

MacKinnon, Catherine A. *Turning Rape into Pornography: Postmodern Genocide', Mass Rape: The War against Women in Bosnia-Herzegovina*, (London: University of Nebraska Press.) pp. 73–81.

Malcolm, Noel. *Bosnia: A Short History.*
(New York: New York University Press. 1996).

Milillo, Dianna. "Rape as a Tactic of War : Social and Psychological
Perspectives." Affilia Journal of Women and Social Work. Sage
Publications, Retrieved from URL : http://aff.sagepub.com/
content/21/2/196.full.pdf+html.

Nettelfield, Lara J. & Wagner, Sarah E.. *Srebrenica in the Aftermath of
Genocide.* (New York: Cambridge University Press, 2014).

Newland, Kathleen. *Impact of U.S. Refugee Policies on U.S. Foreign Policy:*
(New York: The American Assembly, 1995).

Olujić, Maria B. "Embodiment of Terror: Gendered Violence in
eacetime and Wartime in Croatia and Bosnia-Herzegovina' Medical
Anthropology."(1998), Quarterly12.

Phuong, C. "Freely to Return: Reversing Ethnic Cleansing in Bosnia-
Herzegovina." (Journal of Refugee Studies)2000. Vol.13, No.2.

Powell, John. *Encyclopedia Of North American Immigration.*
(New York: Infobase Publishing, 2009).

Stipčević, Aleksandar. *The Illyrians-History and Culture* (Noyess Press,1974).
Spahić-Šiljak, Zilka. *Žene religija i politika*, Sarajevo:
Internacionalni multireligijski i interkulturalni centar IMIC
Zajedno, Centar za interdisciplinarne postdiplomske studije–CIPS
Univerziteta u Sarajevu.(Sarajevo: Transkulturna psihosocijalna
obrazovna fondacija TPO, 2007).

Walker, William S. *German and Bosnian Voices In A Time Of Crisis:
Bosnian Refugees in Germany 1992-2002.*(Indianapolis, IN:
Dog Ear Publishing, LLC.2012).

Internet Source:

AAAS - Science and Human Rights Program (2010).*Conclusions: Human Rights Violations, Acts of Violence and Assignment of Responsibility.* Retrieved from: <http://shr.aaas.org/ guatemala/ceh/report/english/ conc2.html>.

Bosniak. *Oxford English Dictionary* (3rd ed.). Oxford University Press. September.

Definition of immigration by the Free Online Dictionary. Source: www.the freedictionary.com. Retrieved 2014-05-14.

Catholic Family Center. *Our History.* Source: https://www.cfcrochester.org/ about/history/ retrieved: June 2, 2016.

Democrat and Chronicle. *Refugee from former Yugoslavia source*:https://www.newspapers.com/newspage/138481099/ Democrat and Chronicle,Friday, September 4, 1992, page 16.

Human Rights Watch (2010).*The Human Rights Watch Global Report on Women's Human Rights.* New York: Human Rights Watch.

International Criminal Court: (2010). *Amnesty International*, 5 May 2010. Web. 11 Dec. 2010. Retrieved from http://www.amnesty.org/en/ / info/IOR53/009/2010/en.

International Criminal Court: (2010)."Amnesty International", May 5, 2010. Web. 11 Dec. 2010. Retrieved from http://www.amnesty.org/en/ / info/IOR53/009/2010/en

International Committee of the Red Cross."Convention (IV) Relative to the Protection of Civilian Persons in Times of War." United Nations(1949). Source:http://www.icrc.org/ihl.nsf/ FULL/380?OpenDocument. http://www.un.org/en/rights/

MPI. European Immigrants in the United States. Source: http://www.migra tionpolicy.org/article/european-immigrants-united-states.

United Nations Human Rights: Office of the High Commissioner for (2010).
    Rape: Weapon of War Human Rights. Source: http://www.un.org/en/
    rights/.

ABOUT THE AUTHOR

Aiša Purak was born in a small, beautiful village called Jastrebac in Bosnia and Herzegovina. She attended Gazi Husrev-begova medresa, a girls high school in the capital of Bosnia and Herzegovina dedicated to religious education. As a refugee from Bosnia, she came to Rochester, New York and started working with the Bosnian community, primarily with women and children. She received her Associates Degree from Monroe Community College in Rochester, New York, in Computer Science in May, 2003. She earned her Bachelor of Science in Computer of Science from The College at Brockport, State University of New York in May 2009, and in the fall of 2016, she completed her Master of Arts in History there as well.

www.ingramcontent.com/pod-product-compliance
Lightning Source LLC
Chambersburg PA
CBHW020354270326
41926CB00007B/429